A NOVEL APPROACH

To
Writing Your First Book
(Or Your Best One)

A NOVEL APPROACH

To
Writing Your First Book
(Or Your Best One)

Jack Woodville London

Vire Press, LLC
Austin, Texas

A NOVEL APPROACH

Copyright © 2014 by Jack Woodville London

All rights reserved.

Due to Space limitations, the list of copyrighted material used in this book appears in the acknowledgements.

This is a non-fiction work of educational, critique, and review material and commentary. No part of this book may be used or reproduced by any means, graphic, electronic, or mechanical, including photocopying, recording, taping, or by any information storage and retrieval systems, without the written permission of the publisher, except by a reviewer, who may quote brief passages in a review.

Published by
Vire Press, LLC,

2905 San Gabriel St #204, Austin, TX 78705
Austin, Texas
www.virepress.com

Editor in Chief: Mindy Reed, The Author's Assistant
Book Design: Vire Press, LLC
London, Jack W. 1947-
A Novel Approach/Jack Woodville London

ISBN 13: 978-0-9906121-0-0

DCMA Agent Pam Corn at:
2905 San Gabriel Street, Suite 204
Austin, TX 78705
Telephone: (512) 476-6006
Fax: (512) 476-0657
See more at: http://jwlbooks.com/takedown-policy-dmca-agent-copyright/#sthash.1nCYZADz.dpuf

Published in the United States of America

"One author speaking with another, offering fabulous advice in a delightful read. If you love to work with words, you will relate to the guidance and this book will make you a better author. Most enjoyable."

— **DAN POYNTER,** Author of SUCCESSFUL NONFICTION, IS THERE A BOOK INSIDE YOU?, and President of Para Publishing Company

"I believe both new and seasoned authors should read up on what makes a novel into a page turner as they're writing for ideas and to nudge their memories. London's A NOVEL APPROACH goes on the list of books I recommend to my students and clients for such last minute prompts."

— **CAROLYN HOWARD-JOHNSON,** Author of the HowToDoItFrugally series of books for writers

"Every author and aspiring author should read A NOVEL APPROACH before they begin to write even their first sentence. London takes writers to the sacred ground of creative writing, where great novels are born. This book is destined to become the new golden yardstick by which writers will measure their skills."

— **WILLIAM H. MCDONALD,** Author, Award-Winning Poet, Founder of AMERICAN AUTHOR'S ASSOCIATION and MILITARY WRITER'S SOCIETY OF AMERICA

"At Editing TLC, I work with clients who range from inexperienced writers to those who have taken the time to study the art of writing. What I've discovered in A NOVEL APPROACH is a resource which will be on a suggested reading list for all of my clients—no matter where they fall on the writing spectrum. The way that Jack Woodville London shares memorable examples from literature to hit home the concepts of writing is truly novel. To me, it is what makes this resource stand above others and why I highly recommend it."

— **JOYCE M. GILMOUR,** Editing TLC, www.editingtlc.com

"…Aspiring authors and old pros alike will find it useful and fun."

— **JOYCE FAULKNER,** former President of MILITARY WRITERS SOCIETY OF AMERICA and Award-Winning Novelist, ghostwriter, and graphic designer

"I wish I'd had this book when I was starting out. I'm just glad to have it now. A NOVEL APPROACH is an indispensable tool for anyone who's serious about making it as a novelist."

— **JEFF EDWARDS,** Award-Winning Author of SEA OF SHADOWS, and THE SEVENTH ANGEL

"Jack Woodville London has stripped away the intimidating mystery of good writing mechanics. His presentation and explanation of the tools of the trade, grammar, structure, and above all, how to use words themselves, is clear, concise, accessible, and engaging. His egalitarian use of examples ranging from high literature to best-selling potboilers is as entertaining as it is instructive. Though the book's theme is about how to write a novel well, A NOVEL APPROACH fills a more important need as a useful reference for how to communicate using the written word."

— **DWIGHT JON ZIMMERMAN,** #1 NEW YORK TIMES Bestselling Author, and President of MILITARY WRITERS SOCIETY OF AMERICA

TABLE OF CONTENTS

ACKNOWLEDGEMENTS i
FOREWORD iii

THE FIRST PART
    1. Sentences: Be Active 1
    2. Paragraphs: The Lowly Paragraph 3
    3. Forget the spell checker — Activate the read checker 5
    4. In subordination 7
    5. Be serious about your writing 10

THE SECOND PART
    1. Research and Accuracy — *In Exquisito Veritas* 15
    2. Taking Your Research to a Higher Level:
        Applying research to the craft of storytelling 18
    3. Planning the story 24

THE THIRD PART
    1. Story Arc: The Art of Storytelling 29
    2. Beginnings 32
    3. Conflict 35
    4. Pacing: The Event-Driven Story 38
    5. Pacing: The Character-Driven Story 41
    6. Chapter Endings 44

THE FOURTH PART
    1. Characters 49
    2. Characters and Conflict 51
    3. Describing Scenes and Making an Impression 52
    4. Dialogue: "We need to talk." 54
    5. Dialogue: Capture the Story 57
    6. Dialogue and the Language of Love 59
    7. Voice and Point of View 65

THE FIFTH PART
    1. Editing 71
    2. In Review: A Slap from the Velvet Glove 74
    3. The Last Editor 76
    4. The End of the Beginning 77

  About the Author 79
  Other Books By Jack Woodville London 80

ACKNOWLEDGEMENTS

Tennyson said, and it is especially true at this point, that "I am a part of all that I have met." The ideas in *A Novel Approach* belong to many whom I have met and read and under whom I have studied, as well as to me. As you can tell from the references, not even all the words are mine. I want to acknowledge them.

First, I want to thank for gracious permission to use copyrighted excerpts from their fine books:

The GIRL WITH A PEARL EARRING by Tracy Chevalier; copyright © 1999 by Tracy Chevalier. Used by permission of Plume, an imprint of Penguin Group (USA) LLC;

Excerpt from THE THINGS THEY CARRIED by Tim O'Brien. Copyright © 1990 by Tim O'Brien. Reprint by permission of Houghton Mifflin Harcourt Publishing Company. All rights reserved;

THE COUNT OF MONTE CRISTO by Alexandre Dumas, translated by Robin Buss, (Penguin Books, Ltd 2006) copyright © Robin Buss 1996;

"Two phone calls and a funeral", from A SHORT HISTORY OF TRACTORS IN UKRAINIAN by Marina Lewycka, copyright © 2005 by Marina Lewycka. Used by permission of The Penguin Press, a division of Penguin Group (USA) LLC.

Random House for DAVID COPPERFIELD by Charles Dickens;

Penguin Random House for THE MARCH by E.L. Doctorow;

Penguin Random House for SPIES OF THE BALKANS by Alan Furst;

Random House for NEPTUNE'S INFERNO by James Hornfischer;

Gutenberg for JANE EYRE by Charlotte Bronte and SCARAMOUCHE by Rafael Sabatini;

Dover for THE RED BADGE OF COURAGE by Stephen Crane;

Harper Collins for A SCANDAL IN BOHEMIA by Sir Arthur Conan Doyle;

Random House for SLAUGHTERHOUSE FIVE by Kurt Vonnegut, Dell Edition;

Random House for THE DA VINCI CODE by Dan Brown, Doubleday Edition;

Gutenberg for DRACULA by Bram Stoker.

These authors and books will help you to become a better writer as well as a delighted reader and I urge you to read them.

We are grateful to the U.S. Navy for permission to use U.S. Navy photo

(ID 101026-N-7526R-243) by Mass Communication Specialist 2nd Class Marc Rockwell-Pate/Released. In addition, holdings in the public domain played a valuable role in this book and I acknowledge the British Library, London, for *Love's Philosophy* by Percy Bysshe Shelley; the Carolina Rediviva Library, Uppsala University, Sweden, for *The Carta Marina,* by Olaus Magnus; the Mauritshuis Museum in The Hague, for *Girl with a Pearl Earring* by Johannes Vermeer; the North West University Library for 16th-20th Century Maps of Africa (Morocco 1634 by Gerard Mercator #4172298); the Museum of Fine Art, Boston, for *Haystack: Effect of Snow*, by Claude Monet; the Uffizzi Gallery, Florence, for *Birth of Venus,* by Sandro Botticelli; and the Belvedere Palace, Vienna, for *The Kiss* by Gustav Klimt.

A Novel Approach would not have been possible without the human assistance, advice, and contributions by Maria Edwards, Mindy Reed, Samuel Joseph, Rusty Shelton, Shelby Sledge, and Jeff Edwards for untiring efforts to bring this book to print.

Finally, I thank Joyce Faulkner, whose request that I write a series of short Twitter comments for budding writers about the craft of writing prodded me to pick up the threads of my lessons and ideas and to share them with others, just as others have helped me.

To each of you, thank you.

FOREWORD

This is a book of ideas.

Apart from grammar, there are few steadfast rules for writing books. Some of the most revered works tell the ending on page one, use unconventional structures such as three line paragraphs or one paragraph chapters, or employ run-on sentences that describe the age of the varnish applied to the wood that forms the base of the bar of the saloon that is on a nameless street where someone who will never be heard from again goes for a drink on a day when nothing much happened. The variety of structure and detail is almost infinite. Nevertheless, there are some conventions.

In November of 2011, Joyce Faulkner, then-president of Military Writers Society of America, asked me to produce thoughts on the craft of writing. She described her idea as me sharing a sequence of "tips" to help emerging writers work through the "rough spots," which I understood to mean "use verbs" and "write good stories." She also encouraged me to make them short enough to post in their entirety on Twitter.

When I began to think of the implications of my task I immediately recognized that there are within my word processor the seeds of literary malpractice. *The Elements of Style*, Strunk and White, is the revered source for this sort of thing. *Eats, Shoots, and Leaves* is the modern classic. What did I have to offer?

While pondering this heavy burden I read a novel, (name not important, if for no other reason than I do not wish to be called out for a duel at sunrise), that was reasonably well-received in the lists. It was set in one of the many infamous little European wars that were prequels to the Second World War. It involved a couple of sympathetic families in a market town that was about to be bombed into history, an artist who would rally to raise money to bring world attention to the infamy, and a small group of evil military figures who were planning how best to go about achieving total destruction of the place as a laboratory experiment to test their idea for a new kind of air warfare. As I read the book I began to wonder why I didn't like it. It was a subject that interested me. The characters had great potential — reckless youths, a left-wing priest, a good-looking girl, a farmer who was wiser than most. But something was missing. What was it? In the end I concluded that while there was a story, it lacked a sense of storytelling. How did that happen?

What is storytelling? Perhaps a better question, certainly for those who hope to make money from fiction is: "How can I find the audience who likes the way I tell a story?" Storytelling is a partnership between the storyteller and the audience. Storytelling is the art of engaging the audience with something compelling to them, using conventions and devices that those readers are geared to appreciate, while keeping their attention all the way to the end. One of the most important conventions is conflict, creating tension for attention. Another is the presentation of characters and scenes that make the reader sense that he knows them, or wants to.

The writer must do more than offer up a theme or subject that appeals to a particular audience. There are so many books vying for attention that if the story teller sits down to write a murder mystery there better be a murder by page twenty. If romance is your genre, you better put some pain in someone's heart in the first chapter.

The novel I refer to above met the first genre requirement for a historical novel but fell short on the conventions and devices needed to make it compelling. When I re-read the book to see if I was being fair, I realized that the descriptions of characters and scenes were nothing more than mere news reports. Senor X plowed his field. Senora Y offered cheese to shoppers at the market. Bossefina swatted her tail at flies. The characters existed, but were not alive. For example, when a young man went to a nearby beach town to look for girls, the pages seemed like the subtitles of a silent movie screen. I longed for images of freshly-turned fertile fields, of nips of *manchego* that teased the marketplace, the cloak of a late afternoon sun that made the very flies rise from the moist willows and settle again into the thick clutch of bristles of the tail of a very sleepy dairy cow.

The book read more like a work of journalism than of fiction. Places were just places. Characters were just names. Events that happened to them and in them were described without emotion or foreshadowing. Even when some were bombed inside the church, they had blood *on* them instead of bleeding. I wanted to feel the raw edge of skin on the arm that a few seconds before had been carrying votives but now was leaching blood, or to have a sense of being seared alive with a stoking iron while at the same moment thinking it must be someone else's arm since it could not be happening to me.

For almost two years I dutifully pecked away, pleasing some, annoying others. In the very first and not too verbose installment of *A Novel Approach* for Joyce I wrote my first great piece of advice: read authors you like, then analyze why you like their work. My lesson sprang from a fiction workshop I attended in 2004 at the University of Pennsylvania where Jennifer Egan was presenting. Someone asked her how in her novel *Look at Me* she had been able to say so much in just a couple of paragraphs. Her answer: "It's not a secret. It's all there on the page in front of you…" I'm pretty sure she wasn't inviting plagiarism; she was saying that the secret to writing is not a secret. It is reading, then studying, then composing, then story telling.

Do you like the way a particular author has with words, clever and crisp, or with subjects, cowboys or spies or valor in combat? History, or historical fiction? On careful study, you will see that the books or authors you like have a way of writing a sentence that becomes a paragraph, a cadence in the structure that weaves for you, the reader, something appealing. Prop open one of their books, find a passage you like, then turn on your word processor and try to compose a sentence of prose in the same cadence that your favorite author has done. Try to compose a couple of lines of dialogue that evoke the speech patterns that appeal to you — not the words, but the patterns. Write a paragraph, then another. Stay with it until your mind thinks, however briefly, in those patterns.

It sounds like work, and it is, but — you can do this. And, you have to admit, you must love to read or you wouldn't be writing.

There it is: the secret to writing is to go read what someone else has written, then try to be like her/him. As simplistic as it sounds, that advice is to take a creative writing class but, in the process, to design your own curriculum. My library is bursting with every word written by Evelyn Waugh. I have tried for many years to recreate the tone and cadence and sheer joy of the pages from *Brideshead Revisited* wherein Rex Mottram takes catechism classes in order to be able to climb his way up the social ladder to marry Lady Julia Flyte. I have not succeeded, of course, but it has made me conscious of every word that I write and the capacity that each word might have to amuse, inform, infuriate, or evoke — if I work at it.

This volume is a revision and, in some instances, an expansion, of those ideas. I chose the title, *A Novel Approach*, because among the gifts and privileges we enjoy as writers is the freedom to choose our subjects, to select characters from history or events from our imagination, and to tell as much or as little as we see fit to bring them to life. I also chose that title because I believe that with thoughtful effort, all prose can be written as a good story.

Among the devices and conventions that make for good story telling is the concept of the story arc. Story arc consists of an engaging beginning to draw the reader in, describing the catastrophe [conflict] that makes it a story, and then composing the elements that resolve the catastrophe in a way that makes the reader a part of the tale. If successful, you will have filled your readers with imagery and beliefs that evoke their own experiences, fears, and memories, and vests in them the need to know how it comes out. This is the essence of all writing, be it literature, science fiction, journalism, essays, or poetry.

If you are reading this, or still reading this, you are looking for some ideas that will help you write your first book, or your best one. I hope these ideas move your work along. The first two of these ideas, however, aren't mine but are the reflections of every serious novelist I know and of those under whom I have studied.

First: what is your story? You must know your story. Elmore Leonard wrote ten rules of fiction that concluded with the most important: "Try to leave out the parts that readers tend to skip." In *Gone with the Wind*, Margaret Mitchell's story was not Scarlett chasing Ashley, or Tara, or Rhett, or even prosperity; it was chasing something that was long gone, a way of life that was unsustainable, the Old South as a modern feudal state. For Tolkien, Frodo's story was not finding Mordor so that he could throw the ring into the fire, but finding Frodo.

Second: Who is your audience? Hemingway said that in every man there is one war, one woman, and one book. (Hemingway had at least three wars, nineteen books, and an unknown collection of women). But if, like Harper Lee, you have just one book in you, ask yourself candidly who you have in mind when you close your eyes and see the faces of your readers. The hardest deceits are those practiced on ourselves, the failure to recognize that the story you want to share is for an audience of five hundred people rather than the best-seller lists. Take pride in the fact you have a story that you want to share with five hundred people, not remorse in being someone other than Hemingway. And if you set out to be the next Hemingway or Lee, you have the duty to write the very best book that you can write.

The art is not in selling books. In a time of change, when it is possible to sell on an electronic reader more copies of a recycled idea about the un-dead than Bram Stoker's *Dracula* sold in print in over one hundred years, the challenge is to be a writer, not a recycled salesman with a laptop.

The art is in the craft. The art is in writing the best story that you can write. Can I teach you how to become a storyteller? No. But I do know that you can learn to become a storyteller.

In the end, *A Novel Approach* is ideas, not a "how to" book. I hope it gives you ideas that inspire and help your writing and that you will come to agree that the story you want to write can be written with superb clarity and skill. I know you do not want to write a lesser work than you have the capacity to write — you want to write the best. With that in mind, I have thrown in a few exercises for you to try… and a few puns, for which I apologize in advance.

So, let's get started.

THE FIRST PART

Getting Started — Little Things

1. Sentences: Be Active

Avoid to the point of death writing sentences in the passive voice. They are the number one reason why manuscripts are rejected, why contests are lost and books folded and closed within the first twenty pages. They also lead to migraines, short legs, and small children who cross the street to avoid contact with the author. Why? Because they are hard to read. They are not clear. Instead, write sentences in the active voice rather than in the passive voice:

1.) Write an object word, such as a noun.

2.) Write a verb.

3.) Make them agree.

It's that simple.

What does a passive sentence look like? In general, the passive voice contains a verb linked to an auxiliary form of "to be," and generally causes confusion on who is doing what, if anything. In a passive sentence the subject *receives* the action rather than causes the action. For example:

"To the gathering of officers the plan was outlined."

Who outlined what and to whom? With some effort a reader can figure out that there was a plan and that it was outlined. Whether it was outlined to a gathering or to officers is less clear. Unless you intend to be mysterious (for no apparent reason), you have made the reader work to understand what is being said. When you conceal the subject this way, you have interrupted the flow of the reading experience.

There may be times when passive voice is intended but that must be a conscious decision on your part. You must know the difference between active and passive voice. Start out by writing a sentence that contains a direct object and a verb. Check to see if your action word is a participle, especially a present participle that modifies a noun.

Passive: "Being lost already, it was better to stop."

Active: "He decided it was better to stop since he was lost."

To be sure, being passive has its place (it just did), usually to hide the subject (I just did). But it is dangerous to write in the passive voice because the absence of a direct object makes the meaning of the sentence unclear (I just did both, in one sentence).

A good time to go passive is when you want to hide someone or obscure something from the reader:

"The map being hand-drawn did not bother her, but being lost did. 'Am I being misled intentionally, and by whom?' she asked herself."

We know that there is a map, that she followed it, that she got lost, that she inveighed self-doubt, and that she began to worry that someone was misleading her. Every phrase in that sentence can be written in the active voice, but doing so would be journalistic reporting rather than storytelling intrigue.

The bottom line is this: practice writing in the active voice with everything you compose, emails, letters, and novels, until it becomes second nature. Your readers, and especially your editors, will thank you for it.

2. Paragraphs: The Lowly Paragraph...

...can leap tall tales with a single bound, is faster than a speeding gerund, is stronger than the strongest adjective. But, in the wrong hands, it can make your tale hard to follow. In the right hands, paragraphs can become page-turners. Let's be blunt: well-written paragraphs can be the best tool in your kit. How so?

Think of a paragraph as a single idea.

1.) It can express a completely self-contained, stand-alone idea.

2.) It can build on the idea of a previous paragraph.

3.) It can lead to the idea of the next paragraph.

4.) And, with a bit of finesse, it can blend things, although the more unique the separate subject sentences within a paragraph, the more you might consider awarding them their own separate paragraphs.

First, an example, then a bit of analysis:

> "The third Thursday of every month was the best day. Keith put off all appointments until Friday. Steve moved his appointments forward to Wednesday. Henry made a psychiatrist's appointment every third Thursday morning just to be able to cope with Keith's passion and Steve's aggression. But, whether from inability to agree on a different day, a lack of imagination, a mutual gob of intolerance, for any of a number of possibilities, it became accepted among them that the third Thursday was the day they would get together and argue over who had to go to the nursing home and take Mother for a drive on the third Saturday, a filial task that at different times had led each of them to drink, drugs, bad women, flirtation with suicidal thoughts, and frequent review of life expectancy charts. Mother didn't think any of them had turned out very well."

The paragraph above encompasses a single idea: Mother has driven the boys crazy. All the component sentences in the paragraph are working together as a team.

A team-player paragraph has a topic sentence. The topic sentence might be the first sentence. If so, every sentence that follows should refer to or build on the topic. The paragraph may have several sentences that reflect different or individualized concepts or facts but which, collectively, relate to one another and are then summarized in a topic sentence. The topic sentence might be sneaked into play in the middle or at the end to wrap things up. But, there should only be one. Which is the topic sentence of the sample paragraph?

Next, a traditional paragraph has unity. Not only does the paragraph reflect a central idea, each sentence reflects on the idea without repeating it. In the sample above, the individual sentences focus on one member of the family at a time — the three sons and their mother — while saying something different about each. Collectively, why the sons would go to such trouble over a single event explains, and is explained by, the paragraph's topic idea: Mother is toxic.

Finally, a good paragraph can serve as a bridge. In the example, the three brothers doing something together — meeting — is a bridge to what they do — argue. That in turn is a bridge to their mother. They, collectively, bridge to the notion that doing things with mother reflects their dysfunction: they are all a bit crazy.

Now it's your turn. Here is an exercise:

1.) Write out the idea of a paragraph from your story, then write a few sentences to flesh out the idea.

2.) Next, try moving the topic sentence around within the draft to see whether it works best as a hypothesis (in which the first sentence states the idea and the balance of the paragraph 'proves' it) or as a result, (a topic sentence nearer the end in which it sums up the evidence of the other sentences).

3.) Test it. Write the paragraph that precedes it and the paragraph that follows. Each should stand alone, yet lead to the next, or flow from the last.

Keep practicing and be patient with yourself. Before long, the ideas will flow, the sentences will flow, and the paragraphs will lead to your page-turner.

Write on.

3. Forget the spell checker — Activate the read checker

If you are faint of heart, skip this one. It is about a street sign posted in my neighborhood that reads:

> **CAUTION CHILDREN,
> EXCITING**

What's going on here? Is this statement really about warning youngsters to beware of some unidentified tantalizing something? It could be. The absence of a colon, a hyphen, or a comma after 'caution' turns it from a warning into a directive.

Worse, however, the sign also could be about pedophiles who may not know always where to stick their commas. In that case the creep should have written 'Caution, children exciting.'

However, it is more likely that the person who composed the sign made a combination of errors in attempting to warn cars in the neighborhood that children would be getting off the school bus. That message should have been written: "Caution: Children exiting."

Despite, or perhaps because of, the wonders of spell-check and grammar correction functions in word processing programs, errors in grammar, punctuation, and spelling ultimately hole more boats than a renegade submarine. Spelling errors, contractions, commas, and mistakes in word selection are common buggers for writers. They also are the easiest to dust up without the author having to suffer the red marks of humiliation that editors love to scribble on manuscripts. Your word processor will not catch these. It is your job to catch them.

Take a few minutes to read *Eats, Shoots & Leaves*, a wonderful little book by Lynn Truss. It might be about the diet of pandas, who eat shoots and leaves, or it might be about a renegade marsupial that rides into town, gobbles up the food, then uses a six-shooter to gun down the waitress before departing. (The panda eats, then shoots, then leaves....) Regardless, her book is about the devil in the comma, not the least of the imps that cause confusion to writers and readers as well.

Here are a few examples of easily-made, easy to correct errors:

Bee ware. Your in. Sorry for the incontinence. Man eating tiger. And, my favorite advertisement on a billboard at a rather inexpensive motel: 'Free wife for your lap top.'

Be hard on yourself in your quest to make your writing clear to readers.

A Novel Approach

Look for uncertainty in every punctuation mark and synonym. By the time you are ready for someone else to read your story, you're riding will be ready two.

4. In subordination

Write clearly.

There, that wasn't so hard, except that often we make it harder than we have to do. One of the worst creatures of our literary imagination is the subordinate clause, a phrase within a sentence that stands alone between commas or hyphens, and modifies the independent clauses of the sentences. Used skillfully, it can serve as an adjective, an adverb, or even as a noun clause.

So what? The polite answer, by Elmore Leonard: "I try to leave out the parts that people skip."

One part that people tend to skip is subordinate clauses — they tend to add a lot less than we authors think they add. Like fire and money, such clauses can be valuable servants or terrible masters. Unfortunately, subordinate clauses are like soldiers doing push-ups and, if not supervised, easily can get out of sync.

Take a look:

U.S. Navy photo (ID 101026-N-7526R-243) Released

Somebody decreed that the teenagers walking around town all summer with nothing to do wanted for fun so the abandoned movie theater that everybody called the old picture show that was closed because in 1958 it accidentally showed a Brigitte Bardot movie had its name changed to Roller Palace and most of the turned ankles and scraped elbows came after that.

This simple idea — renaming an abandoned movie theater — got very tangled up. Teenagers needed recreation. Somebody made a decision about it. There was an abandoned movie theater. It had been closed because it 'accidentally' showed a Brigitte Bardot movie. It was renamed (there's that passive voice at play) Roller Palace. It (passive, redux) was reinvented as a recreation venue for the teenagers. Lots of kids had little accidents, presumably from roller skating there. There are at least six topics in that sentence, no less than three verbs, and I am still unclear what the sentence proper was about. Was it somebody making a decision or was it about the anonymous "it" having its name changed and "being" reinvented? In a word, the simple idea became a hard-to-digest phrase that looked like a sentence because the first word was capitalized and the phrase ended with a period. Its words, ideas, and topics were out of step with one another.

As more subjects, adjectives, and adverbs creep into subordinate parts of the sentence, the harder it is to keep track of what the sentence is about. These become the parts that people skip. Consider this:

> "Retiring his carriers — and ordering the Enterprise back to Pearl Harbor for repairs — he was promising to stand ready to defend a twenty-five hundred-mile front, and assuring high command that the threadbare Cactus Air Force-which by Ghormley's own count at month's end had just eight fighters capable of intercepting Japanese bombers and which was struggling to fend off destroyers, much less the entire Combined Fleet — could hold off Nagumo's still-potent carrier force."
>
> —James D. Hornfischer, *Neptune's Inferno*

At last count there were six, but maybe seven, topics in the subordinate clauses alone, and only by re-reading the preceding paragraphs and sentences might I get a clear idea of what the primary parts of the sentence were about.

The worst offenders neither complement the subject nor move the action. Consider:

> "Polichinelle, in black and white, his doublet cut in the fashion of a century ago, with humps before and behind, a white frill round his neck and a black mask upon the upper half of his face, stood in the middle, his feet planted wide to steady him, solemnly and viciously banging a big drum."
>
> — Rafael Sabatini, *Scaramouche*

By the time the reader sorts out all the clothes he has lost track of what Polichinelle was doing in them. Why? The fashion clause is inapposite to the action clause, the subject of the sentence, and does not modify it.

So, if really good writers like James Hornfischer and Rafael Sabatini can fall into the trap, what about the rest of us? First, we all write subordinate clauses, and should. Second, however, we should mentally check off a few points:

1.) Do not write more than one subordinate clause into a sentence.

2.) Do not write more than one adjective phrase into a subordinate clause, that is, a phrase that modifies the clause rather than modifies the subject of the sentence. If the word 'and' appears in a subordinate clause it is a good bet that there is more than one adjective or adjective phrase in it. Run away.

3.) A subordinate clause that contains both a subject and a verb should be sized up for its own clothes. Why not write it as its own sentence?

4.) Finally, multiple sentences that contain subordinate clauses will wreck the rest of the paragraph such that keeping track of what it's about is more trouble than it's worth.

Exercise: Go back over what you wrote yesterday. Read it in the fresh light of day. Take each sentence and parenthesize or strike out all the subordinate clauses. Read the sentences without them to see if they make as much sense standing alone as when decked out in your verbal tuxedos and ball (point) gowns. If the super phrase doesn't add to the sentence and the paragraph, let it go.

The use of subordinate clauses that are at tangents to the subject becomes like crying wolf — eventually the reader learns how to skip over what is written such that when a real howl is made, it is ignored. Try to learn from Elmore Leonard — just leave out the parts that people will skip.

5. Be serious about your writing

"What I find hard about writing," Nora Ephron is reported to have said, "is the writing."

There is a difference between writing and typing. Writers produce. Typists reproduce. Okay, that's a bit harsh. Writers believe that a story worth telling is worth telling well. Writers believe that a turn of phrase can invoke a vision, that the choice of exactly the right word will lead someone to think of something in a new light, will persuade, will entertain. Some writers are blessed with a combination of neurons, synapses, left brain cells (or is it right?) that make their words flow onto the page or the screen with clarity and purpose. The other ninety-nine per cent of us must begin, erase, revise, delete, change, correct, and revisit so that, in the end, after many drafts and rewritings, it only looks like it wasn't work. Where to begin?

Your first commitment is to write one thousand words a day. Every day. Facebook, e-mail, Twitter, and instant messaging do not count.

Sit at your word processor and compose a thousand words on the book, novel, memoir, poem, or short story that you are writing. Tomorrow, edit those thousand words, revise them, and improve them. Recast the fuzzy sentences into the active voice. Make the subjects and verbs agree in number and tense and eliminate the pronouns that might refer to more than one person, place or thing so that a reader is able to understand what you intended to say. Revise the sentences so that they do not unintentionally end with a preposition. After you have finished being hard editing yourself, write your next thousand words.

Then, and only then, may you take up the cudgel of Facebook and e-mail.

Malcolm Gladwell dedicated a chapter of *Outliers: The Story of Success* to the Beatles, Bill Gates, and your seventh grade violin teacher. The Beatles played over 1,200 sets before anyone *Saw Her Standing There*. Gates got access to a computer at age 13, then spent most of the next six years doing little else but programming on it. Common denominator: they put in ten thousand hours of work, each of them, before someone recognized their genius. And your music teacher? I don't know about your personal seventh grade music teacher, of course, but such people as a group tend to exemplify the difference between someone who may have had talent, a great deal of talent, but did not put in ten thousand hours and, regrettably, did not go on to perform in Carnegie Hall.

The truth is that composing prose, whether fiction or non-fiction, is a creative and proactive process. You must give it your thoughtful and undivided attention. Practice, dedicated, serious practice, will take your writing to a higher level. It will take time but, if you are serious, you will make time for it.

On the other hand, Facebook, e-mail, and similar intrusions on your word processing life tend to be reactive replies to the postings of others and to be the quick posting of your own news or musings to which you expect others to react. The attention given to such writing tends to be in much shorter spans than the attention given to a dedicated effort to compose a news report, a work of history, a short story, or even a chapter. Instead of such diversions counting toward the time you practice your craft, they just take up your time.

Will it take you ten thousand hours to become the genius that you can be? There is only one way to find out. Start with a thousand words. Revise them tomorrow, and then write another thousand.

That is what writers do.

THE SECOND PART

Planning for the Book

Will Rogers is reported to have said that some people learn by reading, others learn by studying examples, but then there are those who have to pee on the electric fence for themselves. Writers tend to fall into you-know-which category. There is an undeniable urge to start typing page one, line one, scene one, and get on with it. Take it from one who has more than once started there and, pretty soon, ended there — there is a better way.

Where, then, to begin?

May I suggest, first, research and, second, planning the story. Let's first look at research.

1. Research and Accuracy — *In Exquisito Veritas*

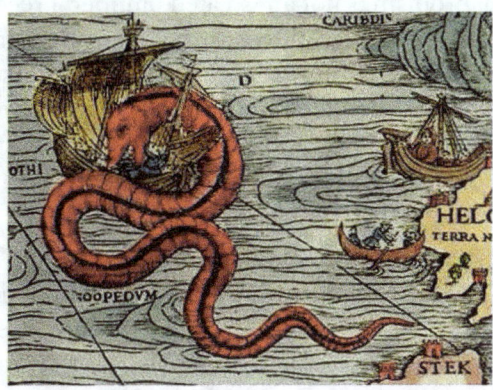

The Carta Marina, Olaus Magnus, Uppsala University, Sweden

There be monsters….

Readers who have some passing knowledge of literature might be startled when in reading *The Three Musketeers* they encounter a passage in which D'Artagnan refers to *Gulliver's Travels*. The dilemma is that *The Three Musketeers* is set more than a hundred years before Jonathan Swift wrote about Gulliver. Alexandre Dumas got it wrong.

On the other hand, no one came nearer to getting it right than Patrick O'Brian. His seafaring novels provide without warning the intricacies of a 'snow' and a 'xebec' and the practices of gammoning and warping the futtocks, details that tend to overshadow the writing that brought such terms our way. *The Three Musketeers* is undeniably a classic; *The Wine Dark Sea* is the subject of much (unfair) criticism for burying a good story in unnecessary historical details.

Is there a line of how much is "just right" in trying to strike a balance between research and storytelling? If there is, how does a writer get on and stay on the right side of it?

Fiction is the land of maps, mistresses, and Machiavelli. It is a place where Newton's laws of physics and Freud's principles of human behavior are the breeding grounds for conflict. It is no exaggeration that bodies set in motion tend to stay in motion, particularly if they are in a bed and especially if behind a throne. Maps lead to treasure or mislead to disaster. As we learn from *The Prince*, it is in the nature of mankind to hate others more for their good deeds than their misdeeds, to despair more from the loss of an inheritance than the loss of a father. With so much conflict at hand, how does one approach research for fiction? Before addressing methods of research, consider some cornerstones.

First, someone will know more about your subject than you do. D'Artagnan's malapropism is not an isolated blunder. I recently read a novel in which a field surgeon raced to a wounded soldier and administered an antibiotic — in 1917, ten years before Dr. Fleming discovered penicillin. Accordingly, a first consideration is the degree to which a reader who picked up your book because they have particular interest in your subject may put your book away without finishing it because of historical inaccuracy. Here are some considerations:

1.) If the story claims accuracy, it must be accurate. If the story is a "tale," a slide in the facts may be forgivable. Remember, there always will be someone who will spot the mistakes. However, the more mistakes that exist, the harder the story is to read.

2.) Some inaccurate details might well be more historical than the truth. No submariner in his right mind would ever smoke while loading a torpedo. Schoolboys might well smoke stolen Lucky Strikes because they believed a magazine advertisement that said their heroes (said loaders of torpedoes) calmed their nerves by smoking Luckies. The distinction here is one not of accuracy but of *veritas*. To write about boys smoking a brand for the wrong reason is a detail that is right because it is so wrong — everyone can envision boys smoking Luckies because of a cigarette ad, even one as outlandish as the inhaling submariners. Thus, a *Life* magazine from the 1940s may not be reliable history for scholars, but is definitely a reliable source to learn what people did and thought in their everyday lives at the time. That kind of research is as valuable as historical accuracy. It leads to knowing what a character would know, even if the character was wrong.

3.) Remember, exceptional research cannot replace good story telling. After once having spent days poring over construction blueprints for landing ships, I eventually proofread my manuscript and discovered that I had written, "He stood at the bow doors that were suspended laterally by four roller-drum barrel hinges each six inches in length and with a load-bearing capacity of…." Great research, awful story telling.

4.) Good writing can overcome doubtful research (as exemplified by Alexandre Dumas). But the writing must be good.

Why are those concepts important? Because the historical story or novel operates on at least two levels:

First, as history, the background details must be based on facts or, in the complete absence of accepted facts, on a compelling mosaic of background details that are themselves accepted. For example, it is indisputable that the almost completely-unknown Katherine Swynford had a long (and productive) affair with John of Gaunt, the now-obscure uncle of hapless King Richard II. Fewer than a dozen documents even mention her existence, yet her and John's descendants are the direct ancestors of every English monarch since the 1400's. By piecing together very sketchy details about Katherine with known details about John, Anya Seton wrote a very credible tale, *Katherine*, about how the two came together (so to speak). She did what would become the mantra of Hilary Mantel: "Question every historical fact you think you know and never accept as final anything taken from only one source of reference. What you learn in the process can take your story to a very high level."

Second, the story should operate as complete fiction. The research should ease the readers' acceptance of the story's internal truths, despite the fact that the story is not true. For example, the Count of Monte Cristo escaped from the Chateau d'If, (as did Tom and Huck's friend Jim). The internal truth requires the reader to believe not only that it was possible, but actually happened. Dumas' research into the thickness of rock walls, habits of guards, and height above pounding waves made believable his tale of fictitious escape. The external truth is that no one ever succeeded in escaping from Chateau d'If, but Dumas' story was so credible that no one questioned that it could be done.

Good research combined with good writing is the cornerstone of exceptional fiction. Cutting corners or assuming the correctness of a fact can lead an author and ultimately the reader off the edge of the map where, as all historians know, there be monsters.

In short:

1.) Do the research.

2.) Learn the facts.

What you do after that is called storytelling.

2. Taking Your Research to a Higher Level

Applying research to the craft of storytelling

Girl with a Pearl Earring, Johannes Vermeer, Mauritshuis Museum, The Hague

> "You are to start tomorrow as their maid. If you do well, you will be paid eight stuivers a day. You will live with them."
>
> I pressed my lips together.
>
> "Don't look at me like that, Griet," my mother said. "We have to, now your father has lost his trade."
>
> "Where do they live?"
>
> "On the Oude Langendijck, where it intersects with the Molenpoort."
>
> "Papists' Corner? They're Catholic?"
>
> "You can come home Sundays. They have agreed to that." My mother cupped her hands around the turnips.
>
> — Tracy Chevalier, *Girl with a Pearl Earring*

This brief passage is from *The Girl with a Pearl Earring*, Tracy Chevalier's novel about the haunting Dutch girl who gazes at artist Vermeer from beneath her blue and tan scarves. Apart from the story, the fact is very little is known of Vermeer and absolutely nothing of the young woman who sat for a then-scandalous portrait, (regarded as an erotic image dressed in clothing associated with impure thoughts and acts). So how did Chevalier learn enough about her to write the novel?

She didn't. No one knows who the girl was. Chevalier instead learned enough about Vermeer and his world to write it, and to make it very believable. What is the general goal of such research? It is to know what the characters in your story would know.

Let's look at a few passages of what she wrote, then go behind her words in an exercise to illustrate how a novelist might proceed to do research for such a story with so little to work with. While this may not be her precise research trail, it is the general method:

Consult general resources, even those as simple as Google and Wikipedia. In the context of our exercise, these rudimentary sources can provide Vermeer's correct name, the generally accepted dates for his birth, death, where he lived and worked and perhaps, details of his life, his family, and his relatively few pieces of art. The danger of relying on these sources too much is factual errors. It is unclear who contributes the information to these Internet platforms, so they are used just to get you started.

Informative sources: Once the framework of background information is in place, research must go to more informative, detailed, and reliable sources. *An Embarrassment of Riches*, Schama, 1988, for example, portrays the emergence of Vermeer's Holland as a wealthy nation caught up in the wars of religion and Delft as a city that hosted aristocrats, leaders, artists, and scientists in its practical canals and divided social classes. *Vermeer's World*, Netta, 1996, provides detail of Vermeer's own art and that of his contemporaries as well as details of Delft and its citizens, Vermeer's patrons, and daily life. This is the kind of background that enables an author to pry out the world in which the story will be set.

Scholarly studies: "*…you will be paid eight stuivers …*"

The question isn't so much 'What are stuivers?' as 'How did Chevalier learn what would be a maid's wage in stuivers in 1665?' This is exactly the type of necessary research that goes unnoticed by the vast majority of readers, but which gives the story such depth that it invites them to become invested in it. Details, such as money and the wages of the labor class, give credibility that a reader may accept without thinking about them. A primary source record of such information would be original tax records of farms, markets, breweries, city taxes, and the like to stratify purchasing power among workers of different trades, a task that might stifle some novelists working in a foreign language. In almost every instance such work has been done for them. In Griet's case, her wages can be dug out of De Vries, *The Dutch Rural Economy in the Golden Age*, 1992, and Saltow and Van Zanden, *Income and Wealth Inequality in the Netherlands, 16th-20th Century*, 1998. Such scholarship is the spine of good research.

'Why so much hard work?' you may ask. 'This is getting complicated.' This is the fork in the road, the point where you, the writer, make a decision: 'Am I writing a historical novel or just a tale?' Wikipedia is easy; tax records are not. If the decision is to do the easy one, proceed to write a yarn and, by all means, enjoy doing it! After all, the result will be a book that might be set in another era and might appear to uncritical readers as if all the elephants in the story's room full of historical details do spout water from their trunks. But….

There are a couple of reasons why the hard research has to be done.

First, there is the 'Twenty Pages Rule.' This holds that if readers don't buy into the story for any reason, (including sloppy history or inaccurate details) they may give it another twenty pages, but if it doesn't get better, they will dump the book into the Goodwill box or delete if from their e-reader.

Next, an ongoing and constant immersion in the accurate history of your story will do more to put you, the writer, into the place, period, and culture of the time than any back and forth hunting for facts on the Internet will ever accomplish. The 'write what you know' maxim will bear fruit, but only if you know what you are supposed to know. If you commit to knowing the setting, culture, and period of your story, a rich and believable world will flow from your pen or word processor onto the pages of your manuscript. Now, back to our process:

<u>Keep track of what you learn</u>: Set up an index system to keep track of your research. Make a system that works for you, whether on 3 x 5 cards, printed bits in a 3 ring binder, the "favorites" bar on your computer, or a combination of them all. Use lots of tags on book pages to find your way back to something important. When feasible, keep the research books, articles, and pamphlets on your shelf since many of them will be constant reminders. The books, at least, should have their own indices and references.

<u>A sense of place flows from a three part strategy</u>:

"Oude Langendijck, where it intersects with Molenpoort...."

A. Maps: Part of the strategy is to find and use maps of the period. Vermeer's Delft, like many ancient cities, was well mapped by the mid-1600s. Detailed street maps of the mid-1600s by Dirk van Bleyswyck and Bleau exist that are so well drawn that one can locate Vermeer's house. The Pope's Corner, the market, churches, canals, mills, almost everything that Vermeer would have known can be located. From them, the author can learn place names and also develop a sense of place. It is disconcerting when reading a story to have the hero leave the house, turn left toward his friend's house, then go on to the park, yet later in the story he leaves the house to do the same thing and turns right. Use of maps reduces the risk of that potential error.

B. Art: Period-specific works give accurate texture to fiction. Vermeer's own paintings of *The Little Street* and *A View of the City of Delft* are essential. Other art, such as Vrel's rock-cobbled streets, wooden windows, and tiled roofs from *A Street Scene* and an anonymous contemporary drawing of St. George's Gate and the jail in the city's west wall are a reminder and evidence that Delft was a tiny walled city. Such art reveals the color and texture of clothing, the arrangement of homes, markets, and churches, tools of life such as brooms and spoons. These depictions will help your story come alive.

C. Site visit: If a place is important enough to serve as your setting, it is important enough to know personally. Walk where your characters walked, look at the buildings they knew and learn what took place inside them. Feel the rain and see the filtered light. Your mind will form impressions from them that become second nature to you. Much of Vermeer's Delft is intact, and going there opens several doors that reading alone cannot do. Hence,...

"Papist's Corner? They're Catholic?"

There are some things that are not appreciated until you personally grasp the waypoints that shaped the story of your characters. Vermeer's Delft was a chilling stew of conflicting religion and morals that means very little when mentioned in a history book, but becomes a heavy presence inside the walls of Nieuwe Kerk, Delft's Catholic church of the 1600s, where he walked every day as a child and was buried — somewhere — when he died. The existence of a *nieuwe kerk* leads to the realization that there is an Oude Kerk, the Protestant one, and that Vermeer's morals were embroiled in the religious wars between the two that engulfed Delft and Europe for hundreds of years. These facts led to the point made by Griet's troubled question to her mother:

> "They're Catholic?"

What was the moral conflict of the time? Chevalier made brilliant use of a moral dilemma, the poor Protestant maid and her supposedly wealthy Catholic employer, a struggle that she used to set up the artist's precipice — painting for patron's money while also painting Griet, a dubious subject in an emotionally charged setting, for art. Such core conflicts can be learned, revealed, or enhanced on the ground much more effectively than by reading book after book of the Hundred Years' War.

> "It throbbed when van Ruijven caught me hanging up sheets…"

Research into the dark side is just as important, perhaps more so, as research into the details of daily life. Chevalier's dark side is a patron, Van Ruijven, who attempts to exercise a sort of *droit de seigneur* on innocent Griet, chasing her around through the hanging sheets. Who was he? Scholarly articles, such as *Vermeer's Clients and Patrons*, by John Michael Montias, The Art Bulletin (Mar. 1987) can shed great light on the peripheral characters in your story because they draw on real people who were interesting largely because they were themselves caught, or at least accused, of doing something they should not have done. Tracy Chevalier undoubtedly found enough in the biographies and monographs of Vermeer's patrons to lead her to write of one of them having a voracious appetite for other people's wives and children. Learn as much about the villains as the heroes.

Museums: The last strategy for reality-based research is to inhabit museum collections of the work and to study personal items of times, places, and people of interest. The Vermeer Centrum/ Center in Delft, like most such museums, has many such Vermeer artifacts. There is an exit shop with books, posters, and similar items that may move research onward. Such places can be unexpected treasure chests of both items and print research. Open air, or nature, museums, such as the old town of Williamsburg, Virginia, are collections of entire houses, streets, barns, offices, shops, mills, taverns, and their contents. These often showcase people baking bread, forging steel, cutting crops, shoeing horses, making cheese, and sewing. There you will see people using original tools, dishes, and implements. An hour watching people cook, eat, and work at everyday occupations can enable writers such as Chevalier and you to write about the preparation of meals, beating tapestries and polishing furniture, and tending crops and animals, just as if you had lived through your story. Be generous with your camera and use your index system.

Remember, Chevalier's revealed details did not come first — they came last, long after research had unearthed support for every fact. A bonus of such research is that it not only gives veracity, it always yields ideas for new storylines and details for back stories that probably were not on the outline when the idea for your novel first took shape.

This is what makes your characters and their stories become real to you. When you reach that stage, the story you write will be real to your readers.

3. Planning the story

A truth: the planning of the story continues until the last galley is ripped from your hands and the printer won't take any more calls from the publisher, the editor, or you. It continues to the very, very end.

A hard truth: writing a book is work. In many respects it is like building a home or raising a child, efforts of love and patience that are hard enough in their own right but almost impossible without a blueprint or the example of some devoted predecessors to show the way. The goal is to write a novel or a story, not to type a lot of pages and bind them.

The lesson: plan your novel before you write it.

There are, of course, no more fixed rules for composing the blueprint of an unwritten novel than there are for the novel itself. Like the book it hopes to become, it may take any of a number of forms — long or short — plain or complex. So, if the question is 'What does a fiction outline look like?' The answer must begin with 'your story.'

Compare the methods of two authors of extremely well regarded and complex novels. Yann Martel, author of *Life of Pi*, writes very detailed notes for each chapter. His chapter notes become chapter outlines. He composes the notes for each of his primary story lines, events, and conflicts, and then continues them until he has completed his collection of chapters that lay out the story.

By comparison, Michael Oondatje, *The English Patient*, is reputed to write spontaneously, by his inspiration and intellect. This sounds easy, but for most of us that approach would be like doodling on a scratch pad and hoping to produce a Picasso.

Unfortunately, many authors I know, and many whose books I have reviewed, profess to the method of, "doing their research, then just writing the book." They often say they do not know what the characters they are writing are going to do until they do them. The difficulty, and it is a real one, is that instinctual composition is inherently satisfying and, thus, becomes its own end. The product, the written chapter or paragraph in progress, tends to go its own way and take its characters into unplanned backstories, diversions, and details. Those, in turn, more often than not, fail to complement the primary story or, worse, lead away from it by dropping in events or traits that do not flesh that story out. For example, in a novel that opens with the news that the remains have been found of an uncle who was killed in combat, lengthy details about getting the telephone call or telegram, about the box in the attic that no one ever opened, about the event of finding the remains, all have the capacity to obscure the story of how the uncle was killed and what, five or ten or seventy years later, it means. The key here is to know what the story is and to write to it, not write the permutations that detract from it. Few of us have the intellectual and inspirational skills of Michael Oondatje. I readily confess that I do not.

So, how to plan for your story? Answer: outline your story, but begin at the end of the story. Work backward to the beginning.

1.) What is the punch line of the story? Write down in one or two sentences where the story ends.

Frodo and Sam toss the ring into the fire. Mordor goes kablooey.

2.) Work backward from there long enough to identify which characters or what event resolved the conflict that enables the story to end. Write down in a few sentences a description of them.

Mordor is a hard place to get to, especially if you have the ring and the ring wraiths are looking for you.

3.) Work backward from there to identify what had clouded or obscured the resolution to prevent it being apparent to them.

Sam and Frodo were separated from their band of friends and fellow travelers. They went to Mordor, the others went to Middle Earth. Sam and Frodo were dogged by Gollum and by minions sent out to take the ring from them. The others fought off assaults on their kingdom, dangers from trolls, and sojourns with elves.

At this point the written sentences will begin to reflect the workings of both the story and the backstory, those parallel events and characters that work alongside the main event, often overshadowing it, and interesting in their own right. Beginning outlines of this type are simple versions of Martel's notes of chapters. Continue making these notes until the story has worked its way back to the beginning.

Develop a system for yourself. The number one quality of your outline should be flexibility. For this reason, many writers use simple 3x5 note cards to write down the principle waypoints of the novel. (I tend to use PowerPoint). Others use separate notebooks, one per chapter. Others use a large blackboard.

The cards (or notebooks or blackboards or slides) can be rearranged, re-written, and supplemented with more cards until the entire novel is laid out in front of you. Once that is done it is time to see whether you have laid out your story, your conflicts, and shaped them with a story arc.

Continue this process until you are satisfied that you know who enters and leaves when, how the conflicts unfold, how they are carried along, and how they converge. As your outline takes shape, begin to transfer your research on places, mannerisms, details of known events, and the like from your research folders onto your outlines.

The more time you devote to your blueprint, the more quickly you can build your novel, and with fewer work stoppages from lack of supplies, labor, or bad weather. As the carpenters say, "If you measure three times, check it twice, then you only have to hammer it once."

THE THIRD PART

Telling the Story

1. Story Arc: The Art of Storytelling

The story is what happens between the beginning and the end. The story *arc* is what shapes a foreshadowed beginning and a denouement that has looped back to it, then goes on to extend the story beyond the expected conclusion. The storytelling is the art of delighting a reader with expectations in which he or she is a part. Take a look.

> Pirate Pete walks into a bar. He has one peg leg, a hook for a hand, and a black patch over one eye, and he wants a glass of grog. The bartender brings it, but can't help asking:
>
> "Wow, Pete — what happened to your leg?"
>
> "Ah, it's nothin'," Pete answers. "I was duelin' over this treasure chest and I lost me leg to a swabbie with a cutlass. 'At's the life of a pirate. Bring me another round o' grog."
>
> The bartender brings Pete another grog, and then asks, "Pete, what about the hook?"
>
> "Ah, it's nothin'. I was boardin' a Spanish galleon and lost me hand in a swordfight. 'At's the life of a pirate. Another round o' grog, Barkeep."
>
> The bartender brings it. By now he can't help asking about the patch on Pete's eye.
>
> "So, I guess that's how you lost your eye, eh, Pete? Fighting on a pirate ship over pirate gold?"
>
> Pete slugs down the grog and answers:
>
> "Aye, we was sailin' the seven seas, high on the Spanish Main, and I looks up at the crow's nest. There's this blasted seagull flyin' around and I stares me eyes at it. The bloody creature poops right in me eye." Pete finishes the grog. The bartender is stunned.
>
> "You lost your eye to seagull poop?" he asks.
>
> "Naw. It was me first day with the hook."

What is storytelling? It is a narrative of setting, with characters, a plot, a conflict, a build-up, a backstory, and a pay-off. Pirate Pete's story has each of those elements. The payoff comes when the reader has expectations — Pete will have lost his eye in a pirate fight — that are dashed with an unexpected outcome. But, storytelling is more than that. It is making the audience a part of the story. It is the audience's, not the characters', expectations that matter.

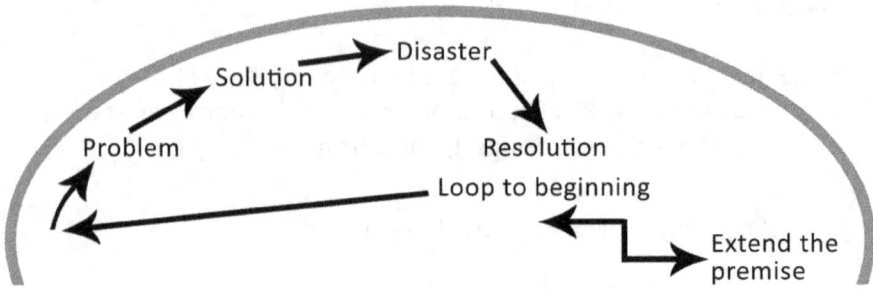

Spend a moment to study the diagram of a story arc. Stories begin when the problem surfaces. Most of our favorite stories take off when there appears to be a solution but, in fact, the solution is a disaster. The story then buckles down to work out a resolution to the disaster. This stage of the resolution may return to an early scene before ending the story.

That device is called 'looping,' the tack of returning to the beginning of the story, reminding the reader of the events that started them down the path in the first place. For example, *Saving Private Ryan* begins in a military cemetery and, after the story of Captain Miller finding and saving Private Ryan, loops back to the cemetery. We then know from the looping how the story begins and where it ends, and, with Ryan on his knees, the premise of the solution – that Ryan has been saved – is extended to conclude with the end of the premise. Ryan was saved at the cost of Captain Miller's life.

Let's look at a second example. *Gone with the Wind* begins with Scarlett and Rhett alone in a room, setting off each other's fireworks, and the reader expects them to end up there. Before they do, however, Scarlett has to go through the Civil War, wreck her family, and suffer the indignity of discovering that stalking Ashley Wilkes has led her to a broken man. In the end, the story loops back to Rhett giving Scarlett's (and women everywhere) bodice a good rip when at last they marry. That is the denouement, the point where all is known except the end. The story then rewards all the dashed expectations by giving Scarlett what she deserves, a healthy dose of her own medicine, and freeing Rhett to move on.

Consider the classic story arc: protagonist + problem = solution, followed by new disaster that fulfills the story ending in the same setting in which the story began. In *The Lord of the Rings*, Sam and Frodo begin in Underhill and make it back to Underhill. However, the story doesn't end there. Instead, Frodo no longer fits in at home. He gets on a Viking boat and leaves with Gandalf, because the one thing we have learned between the beginning and the end is that there's no place in The Shire for an adventure-wizened hobbit.

What makes these into stories? Imagine a bus full of Brownie Scouts, riding in the big yellow bus to Camp Bluebird. Imagine that the brakes fail just before the railroad crossing. This can end in only one of two ways:

* *Train misses school bus*. No matter how much the Brownies scream, soak the seats, and roll in the floor while the heroic driver swerves the bus hard left (or right) to keep them off the tracks, the train missed the bus. It may become a safety report, as bus driver or train engineer gossip, or as parental handwringing, but 'train misses bus' is not a story. Or…

* *Train misses school bus, but….* What if the greatly relieved bus driver relaxes, thanks his lucky stars for averting the disaster, then loses control and runs the bus off a cliff? Problem + solution, followed by disaster: that's a story.

2. Beginnings

This is the point when you should look at beginnings. Draft your beginning several different ways. What is the story? Who will tell it? What is its mood? What is its image? What is its point of view? Compose it as an overview of the conflict and stay with it until you are satisfied, even though as the story is written you will probably return to and revise it.

David Copperfield does not begin with the opening line "I am born." That line turns out to be the title of Chapter One. The opening line is:

> "Whether I shall turn out to be the hero of my own story, or whether that station will be held by anybody else, these pages must show."

So what? Why does Dickens' first sentence matter to you?

Because opening sentences of stories and novels should be crafted with several goals in mind. More than merely vying for attention, they can set up the basis for the inherent conflict of the story, establish the point of view, and tug at the reader to continue. A very good opening sentence sets the stage for the story arc. Remember, the traditional first element is to frame the problem that the novel (or journal or memoir) will present. Consider:

> "First Lieutenant Jimmy Cross carried letters from a girl named Martha, a junior at Mount Sebastian College in New Jersey."

That is the opening line of Tim O'Brien's *The Things They Carried*. While this one brief sentence commences his timeless novel of the Vietnam War, this is no simple sentence. O'Brien has framed the entire story by writing with an omniscient point of view. He has invited the reader to know something that only those who were there would know, *viz*, that each soldier carried something personal as a connection to life before war, and has created a sense of foreboding by writing in the past tense.

Analyze these beginnings:

> "All this happened, more or less."
>
> —Kurt Vonnegut, *Slaughterhouse Five*

> "The cold passed reluctantly from the earth, and the retiring fogs revealed an army stretched out on the hills, resting. As the landscape changed from brown to green, the army awakened, and began to tremble with eagerness at the noise of rumors."
>
> —Stephen Crane, *The Red Badge of Courage*

These beginnings, each brilliant in direct simplicity, have painted a realist's landscape, evoked curious pity, and even highlighted the ambiguity of war. These were not flicked off the authors' word processors in a momentary flash of genius. They represent work and craft. This takes time. What are the elements of these three beginnings?

1.) **They identify the overview of the story.** Each, in one way another, is a novel of war. One, however, is a bridge between war and those who were not there. Another announces that war is too idiotic for anyone to see in its true light. The third raises the chill and fog that each soldier in combat must face alone. In short, these beginnings set a tone.

2.) **They create an image.** Letters, fog, an army resting on a hillside, these are simple and direct pictures that the reader will tuck away without much trouble, to revisit when the time comes.

3.) **They set the voice or point of view.** Two of the war novels are initiated by flies on a wall looking at something, at Lieutenant Cross carrying letters and Private Conklin looking up from washing his shirt to see the huge army across the way. Vonnegut speaks to Sisyphus, god of the pointless. David Copperfield is very clear that the story is about himself, in the first person, and the reader is invited to listen to his conversation. From the outset the reader is part of an intimacy that will continue as the story unfolds.

When is the beginning sentence finished? It is much simpler to placehold the opening lines, then revise them after the story is finished. For example, in Garbiel Garcia Marquez's opening sentence of *One Hundred Years of Solitude* General Buendia faces a firing squad while remembering the day when his father took him to discover ice. The novel is the story not only of Buendia's discovery of ice but also his growing up, his taking up of arms, his betrayal, and his pact with the firing squad to shoot squarely at his heart. All these had to become part of his story before the promise of the opening lines is fulfilled. However, the pace, the tempo, and the voice of the novel are dictated by the opening sentence. It is much easier to write an opening sentence that lives up to the story than to write a story that lives up to an opening sentence. Consider the place-holding a draft opening sentence until the story is finished and the theme is more crisp and ready to be written.

Earlier it was suggested (emphatically, to be truthful) that you should write at least a thousand words a day. Working on your beginning is a good beginning. Write it, revise it, and come back to it until it and the work that follows live up to each other. But first, read the next chapter.

3. Conflict

Storytelling is the art of describing conflict. Storytelling in literature (including journalism, essays, histories, even the Bible) is the art of creating expectations, then dashing them. Take a moment to consider that there are only about six commonly accepted themes of conflict:

1.) man versus nature,

2.) man versus machines,

3.) man versus the supernatural (i.e. "vampire"),

4.) man versus God or religion,

5.) man versus himself,

6.) man versus mankind.

The oldest of these is man versus God, at least according to the theory of creation and the Garden of Eden. The next is man versus man (or woman, or men). Before Cain slew Abel there was no murder, nor did anyone even conceive of murder. Then the world changed. Conflict was born.

Here are some ideas about storytelling and conflict:

First, the pace of writing the conflict controls whether that dash of expectations is delivered suddenly or gradually. Cain's murder was sudden. *The Caine Mutiny* was gradual — a junior officer's destruction of his captain's career was not revealed as such until after a court martial acquitted the executive officer of mutiny.

Next, there are at least two core conflicts in the fiction of man versus man — the *apparent* conflict and *the real* one. In modern conventions the apparent conflict should emerge early in the work. The crew of the *Caine* decided before they even met him that Captain Queeg should not have been given command. Everything Queeg did thereafter only confirmed their opinions because they expected Queeg to be unfit for command. In *Pride and Prejudice* Miss Elizabeth Bennet finds Mr. Darcy to be proud, vain, and selfish as soon as she meets him, and thus he is. The real conflicts in those novels emerge only after the stories are developed and the apparent conflicts turn out to be mis-directions.

Next, the apparent conflict should continue to sustain the core theme despite the development of secondary characters and sub-plots. Mr. Darcy continues to be proud, vain, and selfish. He is gruff with Miss Bennet's mother, snobbish at the dance, and steers his friend Bingley away from

Elizabeth's older sister. The backstory conflicts — will Jane get Mr. Bingley in the end, will Elizabeth's mother find husbands for all the other sisters, and the mystery of what Mr. Darcy did to the dashing Captain Wickham — appear to be the main story. In *The Caine Mutiny* the captain's illogical training orders, his obsession with counting scoops of ice cream, and commands that lead to apparent flight from battle, all confirm that Queeg should not have been given command. In every case these events appear to be the story but in fact are elements that cleverly build the second conflict, the true story.

Consider this: the author must spend substantial time building flaws into the protagonist and hinting at redemption for his enemy. Otherwise, there will be no second conflict. Abel died; Cain lived; story trails away. But the pride and the prejudice that Elizabeth Bennet detested turned out not to be Darcy's failures but her own, a conflict revealed only after the evidence unfolds that Darcy tenderly loved his young sister, had been betrayed by Wickham, and actually drove Bingley back to propose to sister Jane. The second conflict was that Elizabeth, finally realizing that it was her own pride and prejudice that wrongly led her to detest Darcy in the first place, had to decide how to eat the plate of crow she had served herself.

Observe that the presence of the second conflict tends to resolve the first, or apparent, conflict. Accordingly, it is the second one that needs resolution at the denouement. This is a good moment to go back to the first part of this section and review the diagram of the modern story arc. The problem, or conflict, appears to be identified rather early, but resolution of that problem only leads to more problems.

It is hard to find a better example than *The Count of Monte Cristo*. Edmond Dantes was snatched from home and buried in the Chateau d'If for fourteen years, without explanation, trial, or hope. His horrible life then changes course with a daring escape and the recovery of a hidden fortune. The early conflict was thus resolved, but Dantes then proceeded to use his freedom and wealth to weave a vicious web in which to trap and destroy the men who had done this to him. By the end, Dantes has killed or ruined them all and, in the process, squandered his own once-promising life to become as bad as his enemies.

> "I who, like a wicked angel, was laughing at the evil men committed, protected by secrecy, I am in my turn bitten by the serpent whose progress I was watching, and bitten to the heart."
>
> —Alexandre Dumas, *The Count of Monte Cristo*

It takes work to sustain the man versus man conflict. If done well, it may result in an Elizabeth Bennet marrying the person she has opposed for five hundred pages, or in an Edmond Dantes recognizing that his vengeance had degraded until he sank to the same level as the enemies he had destroyed. But, if done poorly, the outcome will be like a horror movie, predictable from the beginning.

Remember, 'Driver steers to safety before train hits bus' may be a close call, but close calls do not a story make. For the reader, something has to change because, once dashed, an absence of expectations is no longer satisfying. Writing conflict takes practice and pacing to create an expectation, to dash it, and then to go on to reveal the real conflict that is the story you have set out to write.

4. Pacing: The Event-Driven Story

The deeper into the story one delves, the more each part influences the other. Pacing is the tone of the novel by which the author sets the manner in which subplots, backstories, and diversions are developed. At some point in the process the author has to make a hard choice and never look back. What is the choice — will the story be driven by characters or by events?

Just as every good character needs a dose of bad, every good story needs a double dose: events and characters. However, when the last page is turned, when the reader wishes there were more pages to read and checks to see what else you have written, when the mind tries to sort out what just happened, the story will have been driven to its end by events or by the characters in the events. Let's consider first the pull of events.

Plant the seeds if you want a harvest. Don't wait until you have written a page or a chapter before realizing that you are in a corner and must write your way out. If you are going to write a flat tire onto the escape car it is a good idea to have a careless carpenter drop a few nails on the road a few pages ahead of schedule, or to send a Good Samaritan down the road long before the escape car breaks down. To say it another way, if you want readers to turn the next page, don't surprise them with something that only luck would provide. Let's look at two examples.

1.) In *The Debt to Pleasure*, by John Lanchester, Mr. Winot was invited to write an unconventional cookbook, reproducing each recipe from the remote and accurate origins of its regional ingredients. He makes notes as he travels from England to France, commenting on the origins of *bourride*. While in the midst of a windy discourse on cheese, something catches his eye; he steps into an *epicerie* grocer's for a look round and studies each bottle, package, cut, and wrap on the shelves, as well as the other customers. Twenty pages on, while expounding on curried lamb, on bouillabaisse, on the delights of seafood in a restaurant in St. Malo, he dines alone and enjoys daydreaming about the other diners. Fifty pages later, amidst snobbish discourses on French omelets and lamb chops, lemon sole and crème caramel, he finds himself deep in France and enters a little church where he observes a couple holding hands as they leave. Sooner or later the reader figures out that Mr. Winot's furtive observations between the *frites* and *salades* occur in sync with his encounters of a young woman who he spotted in the grocer's, later, in a hotel, and again, near a museum, and…. Mr. Winot is a stalker. The reader has been set up, and cannot stop.

2.) Compare that to this passage from one of the most successful novels of this millennium, *The Da Vinci Code*.

> "Grouard yanked his walkie-talkie off his belt and attempted to call for backup. All he heard was static…" *"Au-secours!"* the guard's voice yelled. …*"Au-secours!"* he shouted again into his radio. Static. "He can't transmit," Sophie realized, recalling that tourists with cell phones often got frustrated in here when they tried to call home to brag about seeing the Mona Lisa…"
>
> —Dan Brown, *The Da Vinci Code*

Brown wrote in the opposite manner to Lanchester, crisis first, way out second. Before we proceed, let me point out that his novel ushered in a generally new genre, the historical fiction modern thriller. Those who criticized it as bad literature failed to read it for what it is, a thriller.

Thrillers are event-driven and often do turn on lucky developments. It is no criticism that I never made it to the end of the movie of *The Da Vinci Code*. The endless chase scenes through worn-out tourist stops in search of a killer, a whacko albino assassin, a maleficent secret religious sex society, and an adjustable Holy Grail were more than I could swallow. I'll read the book, I thought, knowing the movie is never as good as the book. I did make it through the book, although for my particular reading preferences it was a hard slog, my mind teasing me with the thought, I'll read some more, it has to get better—this book sold millions. The portions quoted above are the reasons why the book continually wrote itself into corners, then came up with serendipitous lucky finds to keep going. This is not a fatal criticism. The event–driven coincidences of *The Da Vinci Code* were planned, not serendipitous.

The other school of event-driven literature is that turns of events should not be coincidental; they should be foretold, albeit in a way that when they are revealed, the reader might ask, "How did I miss that?" A drop into the mine-shaft should not be relieved by discovery of an abandoned ladder. A surprise lock on the very door through which one must enter should not be cracked open by the equally surprising discovery of a crowbar that happens to be lying around. And (in my own personal view of literature) a couple of people fleeing a murder scene in the Louvre must not get away just because the guard who carries a walkie-talkie can't call for backup when the walkie-talkie doesn't work in the Louvre, particularly doesn't work for the same reason that my cell phone doesn't work in the Louvre. My reader head struggled with the conundrum that either (a) the real Louvre security team has figured out how to make their walkie-talkies work or (b) the author realized that he had written a scene that wasn't credible without the presence of a security guard, but a reasonably competent security guard would kill the rest of the story unless the heroes made an escape and, hey, *how about if electronic communications don't work in the Louvre?* Lucky escape, that. Probably not. After all, Brown's characters went on to discover keys, codes, 24 hour Swiss banks with crackable passwords, Templar puzzle boxes, jet planes, tombs, and remote chapels in Scotland that just happened to pop up when needed.

In a nutshell, Brown's decision to write events as sequences that led from one to the next set the pace and tone of his novel. Lanchester's decision to write the increasingly menacing events of stalking within the cookbook of *The Debt to Pleasure* likewise set the pace and tone of his novel. The writer's exercise is to write the story that he set out to write and to set the tone and pace accordingly.

5. Pacing: The Character-Driven Story

Let's compare Dan Brown, his Harvard symbologist Robert Langdon and Paris policewoman Sophie Neveu, who overcame one obstacle after another to find the Holy Grail, to an equally famous sleuth:

> "My dear Holmes," said I, "this is too much. You would certainly have been burned, had you lived a few centuries ago. ...."
>
> "It is simplicity itself," said he. "My eyes tell me that on the inside of your left shoe, just where the firelight strikes it, the leather is scored by six almost parallel cuts. Obviously they have been caused by someone who has very carelessly scraped round the edges of the sole in order to remove crusted mud from it. Hence, you see, my double deduction that you had been out in vile weather, and that you had a particularly malignant boot-slitting specimen of the London slavery. As to your practice, if a gentleman walks into my rooms smelling of iodoform, with a black mark of nitrate of silver upon his right forefinger, and a bulge on the right side of his top-hat to show where he has secreted his stethoscope, I must be dull, indeed, if I do not pronounce him to be an active member of the medical profession."

In *A Scandal in Bohemia*, Holmes is having one on Watson and, more importantly, on us. It works. But, why does Arthur Conan Doyle's series of coincidences work differently than Dan Brown's? They both involved genius insights that led to the hither-to unsolvable conclusions. Is there a difference?

First, Doyle makes the reader "everyman." He has written Watson in the first person so that we, as readers, see Holmes's powers of deduction just as if we were in Watson's shoes. Brown's point of view, however, was 'fly on the wall,' thereby making Langdon and Neveu comparatively remote from us, people being spoken about, not people with whom we were speaking. In writing from that point of view, it is essential to write patiently, with intimate details of things from everyone's daily experience, so that the reader can visualize the story as if he was watching it unfold.

Second, when Holmes reveals a brilliant train of deductions, it isn't Watson asking Holmes how he worked it out — it is Watson asking me. When Langdon or Neveu gets in a pinch, they or some serendipitous straight man describe the tight spot ('Oh, no — the ancient mysterious box is locked') and one of them remembers out loud something no reader would ever know ('Oh, I remember, Da Vinci believed one of the twelve apostles was a girl! Try the numbers 4578 — those are the secret numbers in Latin for girl'. — I jest.)

Finally, and most importantly, Doyle's books are almost not even about the mysteries — they are about Holmes. They are character-driven books whose personalities are the same each time — a befuddled doctor, a bumbling Scotland Yard inspector, and a brilliant but idiosyncratic recluse who deduces obscure facts from every-day events, all competing to solve riddle-heavy murders. Doyle wrote about characters, Brown about events.

As suggested in the previous section, event-driven stories tend to rely on things that are beyond ordinary human experience. That is what makes them exciting, the rich friend with a jet who is willing to help you flee the country in the middle of the night, the solution to a murder by decoding mythical religious symbols that have been hidden by secret societies for thousands of years. By way of contrast, Doyle never uses coincidence — he employs the very things that we all have, such as dirty boots, barking dogs, ink on our thumbs, eyesight failing due to word processor monitors.... Indeed, Sherlock Holmes' props have little to do with the mystery. Instead, they are written to foreshadow the mental sleight of hand that Holmes will eventually use to solve the case, meanwhile hiding everything in plain sight and then explaining it after the fact.

Good writing evokes in the reader an image of an experience that might be a memory, even if it is a memory of something that has never happened. Like Pirate Pete with the hook and a missing eye, the author has to make the reader see it. This is the heart of storytelling, but how to do it?

One technique is to include details that actually happen to people. Peg legs. Cut fingers. Wounded pride. Red lights. Missed assignments. Black eye patches. Crashed computers. Once a reader accepts the truth of the story, the leap to the fiction of the story is much easier to make. Writing event-driven fiction, such as *The Da Vinci Code,* is difficult because, in addition to detailed research, the story must make the reader believe that the events that happened, to Langdon and Neveu for example, could happen to him or her. With Sherlock Holmes, we quickly believe we could be Watson, if not Holmes himself.

Another technique is to touch base with real events and places, something that Brown did to great effect by putting Langdon and Neveu into such places as the Louvre and the Temple Church, while looking very, very carefully at that one androgynous apostle in *The Last Supper*. The goal is to infuse enough of the recognizable to make its fabric stretch to cover the possible.

In the end, the thousand words per day that you write will begin to inform your own style. It is up to you to use them to set the tone and pace of your story, to let the characters form and the events to happen.

6. Chapter Endings

A good chapter is like a bad treasure map. It will lure you in. It will lead you through uncharted territory. Yet, at the end, it will not yield the treasure — it will just make you want to continue the search.

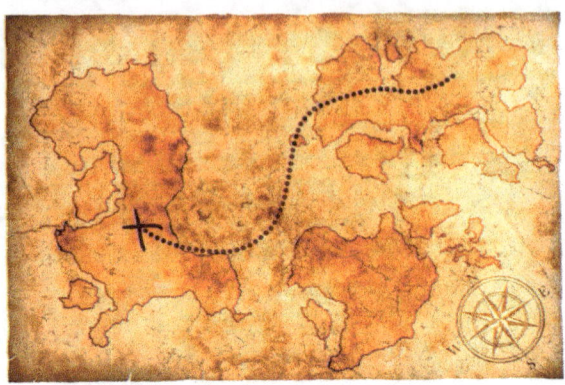

Morocco 1634 by Gerard Mercator #4172298

What is the structure of a chapter? Ideally, each chapter will cover an event, a character, or a storyline that is internally cohesive. Its first paragraphs often stake out the new territory. Its middle portions relate to or progress the overall story by building on characters or events that lead toward the story's resolution. The end of the chapter should hint at something to come without giving away when or where it will next be seen.

But how should a chapter actually end? Should it try to loop back to the beginning paragraphs and complete a story arc so that the chapter is internally complete? Should it act like a cliffhanger *á lá The Da Vinci Code*, a sort of door-slams-shut and no-way-out nail bite? The answer, of course, is 'it depends.' Here are the traditional transition points for chapter endings:

- when the following chapter will change the scene or the setting;
- when the following chapter will change the period in which the current phase of the story takes place;
- when the following chapter changes the focus on the characters or conflict;
- when the following chapter changes the story line; and
- when the following chapter changes the point of view.

Notice a common thread? The author knows what is coming but the reader doesn't. So, how should writers conclude chapters to keep the reader engaged?

Consider this: maybe the end of a chapter should not end much of anything. Instead, imagine writing the concluding sentences as hints of reminiscence for what brought the story (and the reader) up to that point, tinged with hope and anxiety. Or, a writer may plant fear for what lies ahead. For example, dropping a kid off at the bus to summer camp is much more interesting when there's a hint of dread, if the parents are waving goodbye in smug comfort as their child's head disappears among the other kids' heads, yet the child (or the reader) knows what the parents do not, that there is an anaconda swimming around in the camp lake.

Let's look at some techniques:

'Taking stock.' This technique is handy when the story has become complicated and seemingly is at an impasse. It involves a bit of summing up for what already has taken place. Study *Pride and Prejudice* by Jane Austen. After ten chapters of learning how clever is Miss Elizabeth Bennet and how vain and distant is Mr. Darcy, we, and she, are startled when Mr. Darcy appears in her private rooms and proposes marriage to her. He does so, he says, in spite of her inferiority, his family obstacles, her obligation to be flattered, and despite his having blocked her sister's chances to marry Bingley on the same grounds. Elizabeth refuses. The chapter ends with her reflecting that she had misread the situation, comparing in her mind the shock of his being in love with and offering to marry her with her objections to his pride and misconduct. She concludes by reaffirming her decision to say no to his proposal. When the chapter ends, the reader has been reminded of what has happened in the past; the characters are at an impasse. This prepares the reader for what is brewing for Miss Bennet in the future.

'Shifting story lines.' In *The Corrections,* Jonathan Frantzen writes the story of the Lambert family in book-like sections about the parents and, in separate sections, about each of the three grown children. Each section shares a common thread: 'Mom is manipulating all of us because she wants us all home for Christmas before Dad dies.' Frantzen ends his chapters with false resolutions to the immediate sub-conflict that has been described in that chapter. This gives the reader a chance to catch a breath before moving on to the next set of turbulent siblings and their sub-conflicts. For example, in one section son Gary and daughter-in-law Caroline fight like cats and dogs until Mom calls; listening to her demands make their fighting seem pretty good and make the reader anticipate the disaster to follow. Gary and Caroline make up after fighting about Mom, and lead us to anticipate the disaster to follow.

'Change scene, setting, or point of view.' In *The Secret History,* Donna Tartt writes a full chapter in which Richard has spoken with Charles,

Camilla, and Henry about who was where after the killing. Tartt ends the chapter with foreshadowing, the sound of a key turning in the door lock, and the comment "That'll be Francis." This is a prelude to the following chapter, in which Francis becomes the storyteller who adds new facts to the building murder tale.

'Change the time or era.' In *Everything is Illuminated,* Jonathan Safran Foer's novel of self-discovery, chapters end with a clue to a different period in time. For example, after Grandfather brushes his teeth and goes to bed, Alex lies awake listening to the sound of Grandfather's breathing, knowing that both of them were awake and thinking of the same question: what had Grandfather done during the war. With us also wondering about that very fact, Alex and Grandfather then step aside for the time being as the story goes back two hundred years in time and builds toward the present.

The author of each of these examples ends the chapter with a different technique, but does so to build a bridge to what comes next. In short, the succeeding chapters in these examples build on an unresolved question or begin a different storyline while, at the same time, weave in issues, characters, or events from the current and earlier chapters.

Writing is an art, not a science. Even so, the most linear of works, even a high school chemistry textbook, must have a beginning, a middle, and an end. And, like a treasure map, each chapter continues treasure hunt that prods us along between the beach and the palm trees and the search for twelve dead men on a dead man's chest. Plant some clues, but plant them patiently, and never go straight for the treasure.

THE FOURTH PART

Characters, Scenes, and Dialogue

1. Characters

It often is said that an author must be able to write characters who are memorable. But how?

The brief answer is that each character who is truly worthy of being in your story or book must not be just a lawyer, a computer whiz, or a gunnery sergeant, but a real person. The distinction is, 'who they are' rather than, 'what do they do for a living?' If you could listen in when s/he is writing a will or making a final confession — that's when you know what's in their heart. That is the character who is in your hands. He or she will be who you mold them to be.

This exercise was the first serious training I was given at the writing academy. It has been the most successful one for me. For every character of any importance, you have to know the answer to these questions. Since you are their creator, the answers are up to you. When you know them, you will begin to know who they are. (I have used the male pronoun for convenience.)

1.) What is his most valued possession
2.) To whom would he give it? Or, who must not be allowed to have it?
3.) What does he consider his greatest achievement in life?
4.) What is his greatest failure?
5.) If he suddenly became wealthy (or impoverished), what would he do differently?
6.) To whom does he give credit, or blame, for being in the position he is in?
7.) What is the event in his life that he considers to have brought him to where he is now?
8.) What would he do differently if he had the choice?
9.) If he could be omnipotent for a day and save only one life, whose would it be? Or, if he could take a life, whose would it be?
10.) What is his greatest secret?
11.) Who would he want never to learn it?
  And, finally, perhaps the most important of all:
12.) What does he think about when he is alone at night when the lights are out, or on long car drives with the radio off?

Will you use all those facts in your novel? Probably not, at least not as scenes within the story. However, characters who are shaped by their beliefs and experiences become real. A lawyer who lies is a liar, not a lawyer. A computer whiz who steals from on-line accounts is a thief, not a computer whiz. When you do write a scene and your character is in it, your intimate knowledge of that character will come through on the page. They will act and talk in your story the way they would in their own lives (despite being entirely imaginary).

What do you do with this information?

Make a file for each character. Decide who he is and what the answers are to his questions. Make a note of where he appears in your story and with whom. This will become part of the information you transfer from your research files into your outline files and, ultimately, into the text of your story.

When you know who your characters really are, not just what they do, you are well on your way.

2. Characters and Conflict

"May I see what you have in a nice .30 caliber hollow point?"

Characters are no more interesting than the conflict that defines them. In character-driven fiction, the most interesting characters are those whose conflict is that they turn out to be different than anyone thinks they are, including themselves. Let's consider a character who says: "I'm going to shoot that SOB right between the eyes if it's the last thing I do."

If in answering your dozen questions about your character you have defined him as a combat infantry squad leader, or a deer hunter stalking the big one, and their greatest achievements in life are great marksmanship and taking a life here and there, dialogue about shooting something is probably not unexpected. But what if she is an 87 year old nun who has had just about enough of the bishop's arrogance...? Now that is someone I want to know more about.

This kind of character conflict is 'man versus self.' Revisiting ideas from earlier chapters, we saw that what makes Elizabeth Bennet *(Pride and Prejudice)* interesting is more than just her clever observations as a woman who would not be treated with disrespect by a rich man. The Count of Monte Cristo was greater than just the sum of his tragedies. Both of them became classic characters because the resolutions of their stories came with their own realizations of how wrong they had been all along.

This is a good place to restate the classic rule of character development: No hero should be without a flaw, no villain without a bit of good in his heart. Each must have something in his character that is different than our expectations, and his. So, is that nun really who we think she is? Or has she just had a change of habit?

How do you achieve such characters? First, determine who your characters are, as we discussed above. You should be at the point where you know what they have in their heart. The next step, then, is to place them in a setting in which merely being who they are and doing what they are doing is eye-catching. Mothers who tell their children to go out and run around the block, then hand them a pair of sharp scissors, teachers who don't care for *Catcher in the Rye*, football coaches who encourage their players to try ballet, scientists who take yoga classes to achieve inner harmony, and murderers who write thank you notes are the kind of people who act against type. Those are characters whose own conflicts make the story come alive.

3. Describing Scenes and Making an Impression

Imagine that you are blind. Someone is reading a story to you. It might be a news story. It might be an essay. It might be fiction. The page is turned and your reader discovers that, in lieu of words, the author has inserted this image:

Haystack, Claude Monet, Museum of Fine Arts, Boston

What words should the reader say to you to convey that image to your mind?

Or, imagine that you are reading the story for yourself and, when you turn the page, the author wants you to have that image as part of the story, but there is no artwork. What words should he write to convey it to you?

If an author does not trust the reader, there is a tendency to over-write the description. Example: "It was an accumulation of hegari-based harvest product, probably wheat stalk, some fourteen meters in circumference and four meters in height, in the shape of a half-hemispherical ovoid, with shadows of a length associated with a southwesterly orientation at one-half hour after sunrise, blurred by …." Snooze.

If the author does not understand the image, it will be underwritten. "It's a haystack."

If the author is lazy, he will describe it by a title. "His favorite picture is Monet's *Haystack*." (Q: Does the lazy author know which one is his 'favorite'? The reader sure doesn't).

Finally, in an effort to make a reader believe that precision is really important, some authors write what it is not. 'It was not a stack of hay bales. It was not a hayrick. It was not a pile of hay. It was not….' Well — what was it, then?

The craft of writing imagery is at least as important as the art of writing characters.

Understand the image you want to convey as well as you understand your characters. If a particular image is key to the story, answer the same dozen or so questions about the image that you would answer for a human character so that you grasp its essence. A haystack can be a character, especially if it has a cannon barrel thrust out of it.

Write only enough that the reader will re-create the image for himself. I know what a 'moor' is, although I've never been to one in person, because Sherlock Holmes took me to one. Holmes only told me that it was desolate, treeless, boggy, and had a hound in it. That was all I needed to imagine for myself what the scene looked like.

Economize. Except in technical manuals and criminal reports, the reader neither needs nor wants the thousand words that a picture is worth. Do it in ten words, or twelve.

Exercise: Write the image of Monet's *Haystack* as if you were describing it to a blind person, in ten or twelve words. Eliminate words that are not essential to your story and those not essential to what you want your reader to imagine. Organize the words that you keep into an efficient phrase that evokes the picture, but allows your reader to draw it.

Better still, write the scene description at least three different ways. Each time, focus on a different aspect of the scene, such as the haystack, or the morning light, or the indistinct trees in the background. You will see, when you do it, that the scene is much like the story itself — a balance between the main story and interesting backstories. Which is which is entirely up to you.

If you want your reader to see it, you need to describe it. Once you have done so, move on.

A Novel Approach

4. Dialogue: "We need to talk."

Dialogue breathes life into writing. People do talk. Characters must talk. It's that simple. Through conversations between characters, or by revealing the inner dialogue a character has with himself, the writer turns a work that otherwise would be a mere recount of tales and scenes into a personal relationship with the characters, bringing the reader into the heart of the matter and making him a personal witness to an unfolding story. Let's take a look.

Birth of Venus, Sandro Botticelli, Uffizzi Gallery, Florence

"It all started with a phone call. My father's voice, quavery with excitement, crackles down the line."

"'Good news, Nadezhda. I'm getting married!'"

"A joke! Oh, he's gone bonkers! Oh, you foolish old man! But I don't say any of those things."

"'Oh, that's nice, Poppa,'" I say.

"'Yes, yes. She is coming with her son from Ukraine. Ternopil in Ukraina.'"....

"And how do you find out who a person really is?"

"'Botticelli's Venus rising from waves. Golden hair. Charming eyes. Superior breasts. When you see her you will understand.'"

"The grown-up in me is indulgent. How sweet, this last late flowering of love. The daughter in me is outraged. The traitor! The randy old beast! And our mother barely two years dead. I am angry and curious. I can't wait to see her, this woman who is usurping my mother."

"'She sounds gorgeous. When can I meet her?'"

"'After marriage you can meet.'"
— Marina Lewycka, *A Short History of Tractors In Ukrainian*

After you finish chuckling it's a good time to go back to review the boring chapter about the story arc. The classic story arc is "protagonist + problem = solution, followed by new disaster." Then go back over the last one, where the novel idea is advanced that you should know what you are writing about. Then re-read the passage above. You will see that this dialogue exchange is itself a short story. It is divisible by three:

1.) Crazy dad is dishonoring recently deceased mom by marrying a girl from their home country, a woman who is enough younger than dad that she can bring her own son to the deal.

2.) Daughter settles on solution: talk crazy dad out of the marriage by meeting the trophy bride.

3.) Dad wrecks solution. "After marriage you can meet."

(As a lagniappe, Lewycka also weaves in Dad's immigrant English and Daughter's torn feelings).

As the example illustrates, you should approach writing dialogue passages as if you're writing a short story. Even if it's only a few pages long, a dialogue passage should contain what is present when human beings have conversations: a beginning, a middle, and an end, a point, a counterpoint, and a cliff-hanger. It should use phrases and cadences that people use when they talk, which is rarely more than two sentences at a time before pausing for a reply. And, if possible, it should shed some light on more than just the bare words spoken aloud. For example, not only does daughter listen to and answer her demented dad, she also envisions the putative replacement for dear barely-dead Mother with images that leave no doubt about her opinion—don't let Dad get in the clutches of this gold digger! You learn as much about her as about Dad.

After you tidy up your dialogue story, go on and weave it into the entire chapter and then into the book. It will help you platform all that follows, or will help you flesh out what has been raised before. On the other hand, if you omit any of the elements, a reader will wonder why it was written or, at the least, feel as if something is missing. For example, if instead of, "After marriage you can meet," Dad had said "Okay, you can meet her tomorrow," the conflict would have evaporated and the reader would have been left to wonder why the passage was included at all.

A good rule of thumb is, "If dialogue will advance the story, write it." If you can't write it, it probably won't advance your story.

Give it a try, tomorrow, when you write your thousand words.

5. Dialogue: Capture the Story

The principle purpose of writing anything should be to tell a story. Every line will contribute to or detract from what it is the author wants the reader to get. Dialogue, conversations between humans (or vampires, or wizards), lifts that story to a much higher plane. Begin with *"What are you writing about?"*

Consider *Gone with the Wind*: what was Margaret Mitchell writing about, and how did she use dialogue to do it?

During the siege of Atlanta Miss Scarlett finds herself trapped alone with her adversary, Melanie Wilkes. To make it harder on Scarlett, Mitchell makes her attend Melanie's delivery of Ashley's child. At the beginning of the scene, when they learn that Dr. Meade can't be there to help Melanie, their slave girl Prissy tells them to not worry because she can do it. Prissy goes on to assure Miss Scarlett that even though Mammy is not around to help, she knows how because she has helped Mammy mid-wife "dozens of times."

Scarlett is a bit queasy about her and Prissy midwifing Melanie so she goes herself to find Dr. Meade, only to discover the disaster of the Atlanta railroad yard that is under siege by the Union army. Amid the cannon fire and smoke, and surrounded by the wounded who are screaming and dying, Confederate troops are trying to fend off the Yankees who are destroying the entire city. Scarlett does find Dr. Meade but he's up to his elbows in bludgeoned boys. Scarlett finally understands that she has no choice but to count on Prissy. Scarlett goes back to the house where, by this time, Melanie is in the throes of delivery. Steeling herself for the worst, she tells Prissy to get ready. Prissy drops the bomb: she really doesn't know anything about delivering babies.

In this one scene Mitchell told her entire story. On the surface, the birth of little Wilkes looks like a tragi-comic muck-up about delivering a nemesis' baby with the aid of a hapless servant. However, the dialogue blended into that scene is nothing less than a perfect mirror of the South as perceived by Margaret Mitchell: unrealistic promises, the belief that dealing with the enemy would be distasteful but easy because it would be left to others, the failure of expected relief to show up, and then the awful truth — this was a disaster. The leaders of the confederacy knew no more about birthing a nation than Prissy knew about birthing babies and, in the end, they were every bit as miserable. Mitchell knew what she was writing about.

Dialogue can be written to do anything that omniscience can do, whether describing an event or moving from one scene to the next or by revealing someone's true character through what they say. Dialogue is not however, confined to spoken words between characters. As we will see in the next chapter, some of the best story telling takes place with inner dialogue.

6. Dialogue and the Language of Love

The Kiss, Gustav Klimt, Belvedere Palace, Vienna

"In one spirit meet and mingle. Why not I with thine?"

—Percy Bysshe Shelley, *Love's Philosophy*

Romance is on my mind — I write this on my and Alice's anniversary — and all I think about are words of love. For writers, that can be a lot to think about.

Writing dialogue is hard enough without having to explore the minefields and wedding chapels of romance. However, there is no greater source of conflict, nor a more satisfying read, than the story of women and men. So, what do they say, and how do they say it?

In a nutshell, dialogue should sound like conversations people might actually have, not like set pieces in a battle. At the same time, it should not be trite or clichéd, but draw the reader into the conversation and still give color to the speaking characters. In addition, the descriptive scene should be as much a part of the conversation as the spoken words themselves. Finally, and particularly in scenes involving romance, love, or intimacy, lovers who know what the other actually means when something is said are the equivalent of 'train misses bus:' there's not much story there. Love is conflict — conflict with her, conflict with him, and especially conflict within.

Let's look at an example, when Jane Eyre and Edward Rochester meet in the middle of the night:

> "He held out his hand; I gave him mine: he took it first in one, then in both his own.

'You have saved my life: I have a pleasure in owing you so immense a debt. I cannot say more. Nothing else that has being would have been tolerable to me in the character of creditor for such an obligation: but you: it is different; — I feel your benefits no burden, Jane.'

He paused; gazed at me: words almost visible trembled on his lips, — but his voice was checked.

'Good-night again, sir. There is no debt, benefit, burden, obligation, in the case.'

'I knew," he continued, "you would do me good in some way, at some time; — I saw it in your eyes when I first beheld you: their expression and smile did not'—(again he stopped) — 'did not' (he proceeded hastily) 'strike delight to my very inmost heart so for nothing. People talk of natural sympathies; I have heard of good genii: there are grains of truth in the wildest fable. My cherished preserver, goodnight!'

Strange energy was in his voice, strange fire in his look.

'I am glad I happened to be awake,' I said: and then I was going."

Pause to observe what we have seen. There is equivocal physical contact — taking and holding of hands. There is dialogue. And there is internal dialogue, Jane's thoughts, but it is completely inapposite to the spoken words. He avows that she saved his life, he owes a debt, he knew she would do him good in some way and, finally, calls her his cherished preserver. She, however, says one thing — good night, glad I was awake, bye — but she thinks quite another — of Rochester's gaze and trembling lips, his strange energy and the fire in his look. If there is any doubt about her unspoken desire, the passage finishes:

> … "'Well, leave me.' He relaxed his fingers, and I was gone. I regained my couch, but never thought of sleep…."
> —Charlotte Bronte, *Jane Eyre*

Notice: she says, and does, one thing, that she has to go, but her thoughts are what might be if she had but stayed.

That book is ancient, you say. Then let's analyze fictitious episodes of two romantic encounters written by two of my favorite authors, Ernest

Hemingway and Alan Furst. I have chosen almost mirrored stories, each involving people swept up in world war in the Mediterranean, of English women with their men who will be called on to risk everything in battle. We will look at the quoted dialogue of one and at the structure of the dialogue passage of the other.

In the first (Furst — cute, eh?), *Spies of the Balkans*, Zannis and Roxanne are together in her apartment after having gone to a party at which they have learned that the war is coming very close to them and that he will have to go into the fighting.

> "It was very late, not long until dawn, in Roxanne's saggy bed and too much wine, Zannis had intended to drop Roxanne off and go back to his apartment, but she'd insisted he come up for a drink, and one thing led to another. Parties always aroused her, so she'd been avid, and that had had a powerful effect on him… Zannis gazed idly at the red glow at the end of his cigarette."

"What went on with you and Elias?" she said.

"Nothing much."

"It looked like more than gossip."

"Oh, his misspent youth."

"He's tried to make love to you?"

"Of course. To every woman he meeets"…

"Will you, I don't know, will you watch him?"

"I doubt it. The British are our friends. In fact, the British are just about our only friends. I don't know what he wants here, but I don't think that he, I should say *they*, mean us harm." Tired of the conversation, he lowered his head and brushed her nipple with his lips.

"Anyhow, *you're* British, and you're my friend."

She didn't answer.

Instead, a luxuriant stretch and then, down below, she moved.
—Alan Furst, *Spies of the Balkans*

Now for structure: in *A Farewell to Arms* by Ernest Hemingway we meet Lieutenant Henry who is introduced to English nurse Barkley in the gardens of a military hospital.

1.) They make small talk, how odd it is him being an American in the Italian army, how conversations are awkward if things always must have an explanation.

2.) He *asks* her why she is carrying a rattan stick but he *thinks* of the color of her hair, the texture of her skin, her eyes.

3.) She answers that the stick belonged to a boy killed in the war, her fiancé.

4.) He asks why they didn't marry, a question for which there is no answer.

5.) They sit on a bench. Henry looks at her.

6.) He stops talking but Nurse Barkley feels the urge to explain that if she had known that her fiancé would be killed on the Somme she would have married him. She says that she thought that would have been worse for him but he was killed and that meant the end of it.

7.) Lieutenant Henry says he doesn't know. What he didn't say, nor had to say, was that he hoped there had been an end of it.

What haven't we seen?

First, (there's that pun again): what is different between these passages? Furst's description of the couple is clinical, not intimate, more about what they are doing than who they are. Roxanne is 'aroused,' 'avid,' and 'effective.' Zanni stares at a cigarette ember.

In contrast, rather than write what the lovers do or gorge on what they are saying, Bronte and Hemingway write what they *feel*, the self-doubt of saying one thing while thinking another, of talking about walking sticks and salvations while sensing another's hair and the color of eyes. However, note that by revealing only what the *protagonists* think, but never the inner thoughts of the *antagonists* Rochester and Nurse Barkley, the authors put us in the same place Jane Eyre and Lieutenant Henry are in, hearing what their *enamorata* said but not actually knowing what Rochester and Barkley are thinking, infused with the eternal doubt whether their sentiments are reciprocated.

Second, both Furst's and Hemingway's couples speak of a third person, a man who is not there. Jane Eyre suspects there is a female ghost in Mr. Rochester's attic. Why? Because the absent third person is a symbol of the most potent obstacle there is to the onset of love, the question whether there is someone else.

Furst has deliberately drawn characters who are using each other rather than falling in love, having sex in between talking about keeping an eye on Elias. Sex. Keep an eye on Elias. Sex. Who is Elias and, when you're having sex, who cares? Their dialogue and their conduct reflect exactly that.

Hemingway, on the other hand, places in the conversation the fiancé who was killed last year in the Battle of the Somme as the 'someone else' who might never go away — the ghost of that boy. Nurse Barkley says that she did not love him, to her regret, but she is not a woman who does fall in love. Was there an end to it when her fiancé died? She says yes, but Lieutenant Henry will proceed at the peril of her having that boy in her heart forever.

Recall when we looked at *A Short History of Tractors in Ukrainian*, where a father wrecks his daughter's peace of mind with his plan to marry a fellow Ukrainian whom she could meet 'after marriage'? Here, too, Furst's dialogue passage is itself a story, divisible by three: there is a problem, (the relation between Roxanne and Zannis), the conflict, (who can be trusted), and the uncertain resolution (live for the moment, spy tomorrow). Hemingway's treatment also is a self-contained story: his couple meets, they circle one another with suffocating pheromones, and when she says that there was an end of it the reader knows that was hardly the end of it.

This leads us to what romantic dialogue should contain. There are two parts:

Spoken conversation. Here, Furst's Zanni tells Roxanne that she was his friend, perhaps the worst foreplay I have ever read. Writers should write conversations that at least sound like conversations people would actually have. People who meet one another and are on heightened love alert cast about for something, anything, to talk about, as Bronte and Hemingway have their lovers do: Nurse Barkley commenting that it was odd for Lieutenant Henry to be in the Italian army and his asking her why she had a stick was about neither his nationality nor about her stick.

Non-verbal language. This is the descriptive text and interior dialogue (what a character is thinking) that weaves in and out of the quoted dialogue to portray what one of the speakers sees, does, or thinks, or to describe the scene. Zanni is in bed for sex; Roxanne is there for information. Henry's voice may be asking Nurse Barkley about her stick but his mind is drowning in her height, in the texture of her skin, the color of her eyes, all written in the same paragraph. He and Barkley are wading into the real pond.

In the end, well-written dialogue passages of romance, or intimacy, or something that looks like it, profit from what Bronte and Hemingway both employed to great effect: the characters said one thing but did another. Like love, it looks like an enigma, wrapped in a riddle, and is flavored with non-sequiturs that make you curious enough to continue reading, and to practice the craft of writing it.

    Time to come up for air. Breathe in. Breathe out. Romance is serious stuff.

7. Voice and Point of View

Web versus Strand: The Spider's Dilemma

A single thread can take the spider to the prey, but a web can catch more food and keep it safe until needed.

What could this possibly have to do with *A Novel Approach* to writing? The answer lies in whether you, the author, want to take a chance on a single high-risk prey or, instead, build up a buffet of different choices for a feast.

I refer, of course, to the decision whether to write in the first person or to write, instead, in the omniscient voice.

Writing fiction in the first person is an attractive prospect, particularly to novelists who are writing a first or third or tenth book. It is an intimate form that brings the reader into the narrator's life and can make the reader see the pleasures and sorrows of the story as the narrator sees them. It lends itself to story-telling, particularly for murder mysteries and epic adventures in which our hero is on a quest to find the real killer, to find the girl, to vanquish a foe, or to get justice *á lá David Copperfield*. It also lends itself to a voice known as 'fly-on-the-wall.' Dr. Watson's astonished observations of Sherlock Holmes are generally first person fly-on-the-wall tales. In short, the first person point of view has the capacity to be effective.

And now for the advice: resist the invitation. Let's look at two vampires, one first person and one third person. They will help you see why.

Anne Rice allows her vampire Lestat to describe himself, and he tells us that he is six feet tall, an impressive height when he was a mortal and still pretty impressive, that he has long thick blond hair and that it changes color to white under artificial light. In the first twenty pages of *The Vampire Lestat*, we learn from his own fangs that he considers himself to be handsome, a rock superstar, the author of an autobiography, and a Harley Davidson man (beast?). We hear his opinions of New Orleans department stores and men's clothing, of the pathetic volume of edible lunatics and minor felons, and of his lawyer, Christine, who looked lovely against a glass wall.

Compare Lestat to our old friend Count Dracula, described by his foil Jonathan Harker:

> "His eyebrows were very massive, almost meeting over the nose, and with bushy hair that seemed to curl in its own profusion. The mouth, so far as I could see it under the heavy mustache, was fixed and rather cruel-looking, with peculiarly sharp teeth…. The general effect was one of pallor. Hitherto I had noticed the backs of his hands as they lay on his knees… But seeing them now, close to me, I could not but notice that they were rather coarse, broad, with squat fingers. Strange to say, there were hairs in the center of the palm. The nails were long and fine, and cut to a sharp point."
>
> —Bram Stoker, *Dracula*

Between these two vampires, one is a self-absorbed bore with features like a 1980's hair band; it is difficult to care what becomes of Lestat because he cares so much for himself. The Count, however, is seen to act like a proper human, except that he doesn't quite look like one, in ways that are unnerving. Why? Because *he* doesn't tell us; Jonathan Harker tells us. As candles flicker, wolves howl, and coffins pile up, we want to know more, a lot more.

While there are surely better comparisons in the literature, these demonstrate that from the moment a story begins with a first person pronoun, the narrator is on a straight-line trajectory with no detours to developing backstories or complex conflicts. Not only is the story his and only his to tell, but every character is confined to his perceptions, every scene is defined by his description, each event is limited to what he rationally could have seen or known. Every coincidence in the plot conflict must be explained by information the narrator did not have. If any one of those loses the reader's attention, the novel is broken. If at any point the reader doesn't like that world view, the reader stops reading. A story written in a different voice, however, gives great flexibility to the writer to describe any scene, character, or idea from any point of view and leave the reader open to impending change.

Authors almost certainly are the worst judges of what a reader will think of a character whose essence is written in the first person. If that character is not interesting or believable or lacks something that would make the reader care about him from the outset, the author need not have written beyond page twenty. First person narrators who are bores don't last that long. The spider's single thread can be broken at any point along the story arc, from the introduction through to meeting additional characters, in new scenes or in new conflicts. If at any time the reader's attachment to them is lost the novel is lost. The book will be put down (or, worse, a review will be written).

The spider web of omniscience has a much greater capacity to hold the reader. Each character is given not only the gifts of speech and appearance, but also the gift of private thoughts — evil, wise, stupid, mean, anything and everything. The author of *The Hunger* can say what his vampire Miriam is thinking about not-quite-vampire John's impending demise quite independently of what John thinks of Miriam. Developments, such as new blood plasma that might make John live as a dead man forever, can unfold quite detached from John and Miriam knowing about them during their quest for fast food humans. The reader may see what the characters do not. The web weaves every plot, character, and conflict into a layered story that comes *together* rather than merely coming *out*.

Perhaps no better example of omniscient fiction exists than *The Lord of the Rings*. If Tolkien had confined us to Frodo's voice, Gandalf would be limited to a few scenes in the Shire and disappearing inside the Mines of Moria. Aragorn would never fall in love with Arwen. Gollum would be a salamander. Why? Because, as written, none of the characters and their histories happen in the company of all the members of the quest, or at the same time, much less exclusively in Frodo's presence.

Are there any well-written first person novels? Of course. There is no single way to write a novel, and exclusion of "I" as the narrator would foreclose not only Dickens' sixth novel, but Marcel Proust, William Boyd, and Ernest Hemingway, among many others. The moral of the spider web is not that one shouldn't try to catch an audience with a single strand but, rather, that one should do so only after having first learned how to weave an entire web. It is an art that appears to be quite simple, but is represented more by its gallery of failures than its successes.

The bottom line: Budding novelists should learn to write in the omniscient voice. A shortcoming on that score will be apparent in the novel.

Excursions into first person voice can be made by inserting faux journals, memoirs, and letters if it is important to dwell at some length inside the perceptions and thoughts of a single character. With time and work, that device will come too, but until it does, the risk of writing in the first person is the same as the risk of sounding self-important, a confection that loses its taste too soon.

THE FIFTH PART

Wrapping Up

1. Editing

Here is the hierarchy of editors who may have a role in your story:

1.) Yourself — essential.

2.) Anyone you sleep with — very bad idea.

3.) Friends who like to read books. Not quite as bad as number 2, above, but must be employed with caution and in moderation. Friends who read are rarely trained to analyze written works for the presence or absence of structural conventions, story arc, and writing active rather than passive sentences. They might, however, catch a lot of typographical errors. Even if their red marks for grammar are wrong the very challenges should force you to consider whether you have made mistakes. On the other side of the ledger, though, is that friends are put in the awkward position of saying that they like the book, no matter how badly written, to keep the friendship intact, or saying what they really think, at the expense of you avoiding each other in restaurants, moving the children to a different school, adopting sunglasses in winter, and changing email addresses.

In a nutshell, hire a professional editor. Editors are a necessary good, not a necessary evil. Good editors catch grammatical errors, spelling errors, and organizational errors. Very good editors have the uncanny skill to follow the story that has been written. They are able to observe where the author swerves away from the story or obscures it or even fails to tell a story at all.

Great editors combine not only those two traits but also have the talent to recognize how the story can be got back on track. More often than not this last contribution means telling the author to remove tons of things that have been written into the manuscript during fits of research rapture or in bouts of self-love with one's prose. The most honest editors look the author in the eye and say with candor what no one else has said before.

Having said that, revisit the hierarchy above and note that you are an essential editor. You must rigorously review what you have written on a very regular basis. Your review should begin with checking for grammatical and typographical errors. You must make at least a second pass over the entire manuscript to assure that what you have written truly advances the story you have set out to write. You were strongly urged in an earlier chapter to outline your story from end to beginning, then to supplement it until the outline was sufficiently complete to enable you to identify and place in order your conflict, your characters, your events, your backstory, and the main story, all converging in the story you set out to write.

It is at this point, the editing, that the value of this advice pays dividends. I cannot speak for any of the authors whose work or advice I have mentioned up to this point, but I can speak for myself — there is a terrible hollow in the stomach, a gaunt caste to the eye, a bitter taste that cannot be brushed away, a weary and depressive acknowledgment when, after having written fifteen or twenty or thirty thousand words, you read your manuscript only to discover that it does not tell the story that it was supposed to tell. This means starting over — from scratch. Since no one but you knows what that story is, no one, not even the best editor, can tell you how to rebuild it. The best editors can take the story you intended to write and help you to rescue it from the slough, but in order for them to do so, the story has to be in there somewhere. Otherwise, the best editors will read what you gave them and hand it back, saying "Where's the story?"

The story has to be in the outline you wrote at the beginning. You must get it into the manuscript yourself. Then, you must be your first editor. How does that work?

A good rule of thumb when editing manuscripts is to revise three chapters at a time. Consider whether the first of the three concludes by hinting, implying, or threatening some event that is postponed until further notice. The succeeding chapters can either build on that unresolved question or begin a different storyline while, at the same time, weaving in issues, characters, or events from the first of the three chapters. Readers get a great sense of reward by picking up a character, storyline, or event that was hinted at several chapters previously. In this way, you can see whether what you wrote in, say, chapter two, agrees with chapter one and points to what will be revealed in chapter three. But, if there is no break from the end of one chapter and the content of the next, or if the chapter is internally complete, the storytelling falters.

In *The March*, Doctorow's novel of Sherman's march through the South, a chapter begins with Sherman's telegram to Lincoln:

> "I beg to present to you as a Christmas gift the city of Savannah, with one hundred fifty heavy guns and plenty of ammunition. Also about twenty-five thousand bales of cotton."

Preceding chapters had already marched us from Atlanta to Savannah, had burned houses, buried men and horses, freed slaves, torched plantations, pillaged women, and created baggage train camp followers. The capture of Savannah intact and with spoils was a welcome relief. Doctorow then wrote a chapter with Sherman in the captured Savannah, planning to attack up the Carolinas, where the novel will lead. But, in concluding that chapter, he told us that:

> "At the end of the evening Sherman went to his rooms mellow with wine and feeling more relaxed than he had in days. He was humming the overture to *The Flying Dutchman*. Some newspapers were newly arrived from Ohio. He lit a cigar and, expecting to amuse himself with the local gossip, sat back and read in the Columbus, Ohio, *Times*, that Charles Sherman, the six-month-old son of General and Mrs. William Tecumseh Sherman, had died of the croup."

Doctorow's map of impersonal death and destruction had led us to Savannah, as we knew it would. It points toward the end of the war, as we know it will. But, in this chapter, Doctorow reveals that the war that Sherman had taken to the South had taken Sherman as well. The future chapters lead to the prize, the end of the war, but even he began to pay the price. He, however, and we, would go on.

Writing is an art, not a science. Even so, the most linear of works, such as a high school chemistry textbook, must have a beginning, a middle, and an end. It is that middle of the treasure hunt that reminds us that between the beach and the palm trees there are twelve dead men on a dead man's chest. That middle is best seen when you edit it first: three chapters at a time.

2. In Review: A Slap from the Velvet Glove

"That's not writing; that's typing."

Reviews, and reviewers, can be cruel. Imagine, for a moment, that you have written a novel or story. Imagine for a second moment, that a reviewer whose opinion you value wrote that line about your masterpiece. Such reviews and comments are slaps from the life force of those fountains of approval, which authors crave to help spread the word about what took three years (or more) and countless wads of paper to turn into a novel. Jack Kerouac was on the wrong end of that line, one spoken by Truman Capote but, nevertheless, a cruel review. So, how to avoid such a dagger? A good review starts, to be candid, with a good book.

If there is anything more contentious than the relationship between author and critic it would be the relationship between author and book reviewer. So, as an author, you have to be honest about what you hope for in a good review. In truth, you want it to be about the book, not (much) about you the author, and not (ever) about the reviewer. Live your life accordingly.

So, what does one of those well-written reviews look like? It's pretty simple, really. A well-composed review has about four stages.

> **1.) The lead line**: The review should state not only the title and author but also the publisher, ISBN, and price of the book. If you are writing the review, this doesn't seem like too much to ask since the book is sitting right there in front of you.
>
> **2.) The reader line**: Reviews should help readers decide whether to read the book. A reader line moves that along by placing the book within a field or genre, such as "*Army at Dawn* is a history of the fledgling United States Army in the European theater of World War II." "*A Debt to Pleasure* is black humor, a novel of revenge of the kind dreamed of by younger brothers everywhere." Most readers know after just that introduction whether to stop or continue.

Now, for a bit of chicken-egg: The next two components should emerge from the murk of every review but which comes first is for the reviewer to decide.

> **3.) (or 4). The summary line**: The review should summarize the book in sufficient detail to provide a fair glance of what lurks between the covers. Reviews of novels should describe the setting, scene, principal characters, and at least a hint of the conflict within the story. Reviews of non-fiction work should describe the subject matter.

4.) (or 3). **The contribution line:** This bit separates the men from the boys, the Brownies from the Girl Scouts, the Cessnas from the space shuttles: what does the book add to the literature in the field? Mention at least a couple of the leading titles in the genre and compare the reviewed book to them. Is the book a new addition to the author's body of work? List some of the author's other works and discuss how the new one fits in with the author's known style, merits, or the nature of his (her) past writings. This means, of course, that the reviewer has to at least read something from the leading titles in the genre or, (dare I ask too much?) read some of the author's other works, preferably before writing the review. This is often referred to as the part of the review process that is 'separating the vacuum cleaner from that which merely sucks.' Even so, if the review is to have any credibility, it should be plain that the reviewer knows what he's talking about.

At this point it should occur to you that a well-written review of your story will raise those same questions about your novel and, perhaps, yourself. Where, for example, does your story fall within the genre? Does it add to the literature? Does it mark your progress as an author? These are good questions to have in the back of your mind throughout your creative process, one more layer of anxiety to accommodate for some nasty-minded (or brilliant) reviewer in the future.

A couple of don'ts: It isn't too hard to see which reviews are honest efforts and which have been written as favors. Don't further devalue reviews by writing one-line summaries such as 'Great read,' 'S/he can really write!' or (my favorite) '5 stars!' Amazon has already done enough to make every word ever uploaded into a gold star on someone's path to the Pulitzer. The review should be about the book, and not tell the reader of the review that s/he should buy the book (or pass over it) because the reviewer says to "trust him."

What about the nasty stuff? Reviewers are, generally, inferior to the rest of us. To be perfectly honest, no review ever gets it entirely right. But, if you are called on to write one, don't back away from critiquing the weaknesses, the hanging story lines, the unexplained or undeveloped characters, and the outright mistakes. Criticism is painful, but not fatal.

In the end, keep in mind that it's not supposed to be personal. A nasty review that is personal looks more like this one, attributed to a writer for a New York paper about a book by Ilka Chase:

"I enjoyed reading your book. Who wrote it for you?"

"I wrote it myself," she replied. "Who read it to you?"

Sometimes the velvet glove slaps back.

3. The Last Editor

The last editor is your reader.

From among our hierarchy of editors, ourselves, our mates, our friends, and our professional editors, this is the one for whom you write. I suggested earlier that storytelling is something of a partnership between the author and the reader. The art of storytelling is to engage the reader by use of conventions and devices to enter the world you create and to stay in that world until you have resolved the conflict that did not exist before you wrote about it.

The reader will be your harshest editor, the one who will put your book down if you don't keep your promise, if there is no murder in the mystery by page 20, no bodice ripe for ripping by the end of the first chapter, no dread of the headsman's block by the time Anne Boleyn first sees Henry VIII riding into her father's castle.

When you read your prose, edit your manuscript, and revise your story for the fifteenth time, remember yourself as a reader. How many grammatical mistakes do you forgive before you put down a badly-edited book? How many clichés? How many pages do you read before you close a volume that has no apparent plot or whose characters are not interesting? Your readers will be no more kind to you than you are to the books you dump in the Goodwill bin.

It is for your harshest critic that you decided to write your story. The pride you take in crafting it will come through your pages. Know your story, know your audience, and take all the time needed to bring the two together.

4. The End of the Beginning

Final Exercise: write your book.

I hope these ideas are helpful. As simple as they are and as simple as they sound, they all come together in a complex but rewarding pattern. Know your story and tell it. Employ conventions, such as the story arc and looping, to write it. Employ devices, such as the development of characters and point of view to sharpen the conflict. Write the very best book that you can.

That is the novel approach.

Jack Woodville London
Austin, Texas, USA 2014

About the Author

Jack Woodville London studied the craft of fiction at the Academy of Fiction, St. Céré, France and at Oxford University. He was the first Author of the Year of the Military Writers Society of America.

His French Letters novels are widely praised for their portrayal of America in the 1940s, both at home and in the Second World War, and as Americans evolved from the experience of that war into the consumer society of the baby boom generation. The first book, *Virginia's War,* was a Finalist for Best Novel of the South and the Dear Author 'Novel with a Romantic Element' contests. The second volume, *Engaged in War,* won the silver medal for general fiction at the London Book Festival, among other awards. *Children of a Good War,* the final book in that series, won the Foreword Review award for the best novel of 2018 in war and military fiction and was included in the Kirkus Reviews Best Books of 2018 Indie Edition.

This book, *A Novel Approach,* won the E-Lit Gold Medal for non-fiction in 2015.

Jack also is the author of several published articles on the craft of writing and on early 20th century history.

His work in progress is *Shades of the Deep Blue Sea,* a mystery-adventure novel about two sailors and a girl, (and cannibals…) set on a Pacific island World War II.

He lives in Austin, Texas. Visit him at jwlbooks.com or contact him at jack@jackwlondon.com.

Other Books By Jack Woodville London

French Letters: Virginia's War
Virginia's War is a novel of one woman's battle to lead her own life on the American home front during World War II, finalist for Best Novel of the South and Romantic Novels with a Twist.
ISBN-13: 978-0981597508 (paperback)
ASIN: B0030ZRWXA (Kindle)

French Letters: Engaged in War
Engaged in War, a parallel story to Virginia's War, is a novel of a naïve army doctor thrown into the war during the D-Day allied invasion, winner of the Indie Excellence Award and silver prizes in the London Book Festival and the Stars and Flags competitions.
ISBN-13: 978-0982120712 (paperback)
ASIN: B0041D8X88 (Kindle)

French Letters: Children of a Good War
Children of a Good War, winner of Foreword Review's 2018 gold medal for military and war fiction of the year, is the crown jewel in Jack Woodville London's French Letters Trilogy.
ISBN-13: 978-0990612186 (paperback)
ASIN: B07H9KF9Q5 (Kindle)